Jolson & COMPANY

A Musical Play by

Stephen Mo Hanan & Jay Berkow

SAMUEL FRENCH, INC.

45 West 25th Street
NEW YORK 10010
LONDON

7623 Sunset Boulevard
HOLLYWOOD 90046
TORONTO

Printed in the U.S.A.
0 573 62954 4

IMPORTANT BILLING AND CREDIT REQUIREMENTS

All producers of *JOLSON & COMPANY must* give credit to the Authors of the Work in all programs distributed in connection with performances of the Work, and in all instances in which the title of the Work appears for the purposes of advertising, publicizing or otherwise exploiting a production thereof, including, without limitation, programs, souvenir books and playbills. The names of the Authors must appear on a separate line in which no other matter appears, and *must* be in size of type not less than 50% of the size used for the title of the Work. In addition, the following *must* appear in all programs distributed in connection with performances of the play:

Swanee by Irving Caesar and George Gershwin
A Bird in a Gilded Cage by Arthur J. Lamb and Harry von Tilzer
I'm Sitting on Top of the World by Ray Henderson, Joe Young and Sam Lewis*
The Little Victrola by Billy Murray and Norbert Roscoe
You Made Me Love You by James Monaco and Joseph McCarthy
Where Did Robinson Crusoe Go with Friday on Saturday Night? by George Meyer, Joe Young and Sam Lewis
California Here I Come by Joseph Meyer, B.G. DeSylva and Al Jolson**
Sonny Boy by Ray Henderson, Lew Brown and B.G. DeSylva***
When the Red, Red Robin Comes Bob-Bob-Bobbin' Along by Harry M. Woods****
My Mammy by Walter Donaldson, Joe Young and Sam Lewis
Toot Toot Tootsie by Gus Kahn, Ernie Erdman and Dan Russo
Hello Central Give Me No Man's Land by Jean Schwartz, Joe Young and Sam Lewis
Rock-a-Bye Your Baby with a Dixie Melody by Jean Schwartz, Joe Young and Sam Lewis
April Showers by B.G. DeSylva and Louis Silvers

*Used by permission from Ray Henderson Music Co., EMI Feist Catalog, Inc. and Warock Corp.
**Used by permission from The Songwriters Guild, Jo Ro Music and Warner Chappell & Co., Inc.
***Used by permission from The Songwriter's Guild, Warner Chappell & Co., Inc. and Ray Henderson Music Co.
****Used by permission from The Songwriter's Guild

THEATRE AT SAINT PETER'S

Janet Hayes Walker, Founding Artistic Director, 1925-1997

ONE OF A KIND FOR THIRTY YEARS

James Morgan, *Artistic Director*
Robert A. Buckley, *Managing Director*

PRESENTS

Jolson & Co.

A NEW MUSICAL PLAY

By **Stephen Mo Hanan & Jay Berkow**

With

Nancy Anderson · Robert Ari
and **Stephen Mo Hanan** *as Al Jolson*

Scenic Design **James Morgan**
Costume Design **Gail Baldoni**
Lighting Design **Annmarie Duggan**
Casting **Joseph McConnell**
Press Representative **Keith Sherman & Associates**
Production Stage Manager **Jack Gianino**

Music Direction **Peter Larson**
Directed by **Jay Berkow**

CHARACTERS

The play can be performed by various sized casts. The original production was performed by three actors playing the following roles:

ACTOR ONE: (50s) Plays Jolson throughout

ACTOR TWO: (30s-50s) Plays Barry Gray, Poppa, Harry Jolson, Dockstader, Lloyd Bacon, Chuck DiAngelo, Col. Webster, Harry Cohn and Morris Stoloff

ACTOR THREE: (20s) Plays Nancy, Naomi, Mae, Ethel, Josephine, Ruby, Martha and Erle

SCENE

The stage of the Winter Garden Theater
and various locales from Jolson's past.

TIME

December, 1949.

MUSICAL NUMBERS

Swanee
   by Irving Caesar & George Gershwin

A Bird in a Gilded Cage
   by Arthur J. Lamb & Harry von Tilzer

I'm Sitting on Top of the World
   by Ray Henderson, Joe Young & Sam Lewis

The Little Victrola
   by Billy Murray & Norbert Roscoe

You Made Me Love You
   by James Monaco & Joseph McCarthy

Where Did Robinson Crusoe Go with Friday on Saturday Night?
   by George Meyer, Joe Young & Sam Lewis

California Here I Come
   by Joseph Meyer, B. G. DeSylva & Al Jolson

Sonny Boy
   by Ray Henderson, Lew Brown & B. G. DeSylva

When the Red Red Robin Comes Bob-Bob-Bobbin' Along
   by Harry M Woods

My Mammy
   by Walter Donaldson, Joe Young & Sam Lewis

Toot Toot Tootsie
   by Gus Kahn, Ernie Erdman & Dan Russo

Hello Central Give Me No Man's Land
   by Jean Schwartz, Joe Young & Sam Lewis

Rock-a-Bye Your Baby with a Dixie Melody
   by Jean Schwartz, Joe Young & Sam Lewis

You Made Me Love You (Reprise)

April Showers
   by B. G. DeSylva & Louis Silvers

You Made Me Love You (Finale)

ACT I

(The stage of the Winter Garden Theatre. BARRY GRAY is seated at a table with a vintage microphone.)

NANCY. Hello, ladies and gentlemen, good evening. It's exactly 30 seconds to air time so if you could please take your seats. Welcome to this very special live Barry Gray show with our special guest you-know-who. We'd like to thank the Shubert brothers for permitting us the use of the historic Winter Garden Theatre. Let me remind you we're broadcasting live to a national audience so please respond accordingly when the On-Air sign is illuminated, and if you're carrying anything that could make an unwanted noise, please don't let it. Just a moment, and that's my signal. Welcome to At Ease, going live in five, four, three, two ....

(A studio sign lights up reading "ON THE AIR." Music cue—Barry Gray Theme. NANCY exits.)

BARRY. Ladies and gentlemen, good evening. This is Barry Gray, and you're listening to At Ease, a program of the Mutual Broadcasting System, Station WOR New York. If you feel a buzz coming over the wires, don't adjust your radio, it's just a certain excess electricity that always accompanies tonight's special guest. And our live audience is larger than usual, because we are broadcasting tonight not from the studio but from the stage of one of the great Broadway theaters, the Winter Garden—

JOLSON. *(From the wings.)* Bring me out already.

BARRY. Almost there, Al, hold tight.

JOLSON. *(As before.)* Lemme at 'em!

BARRY. In a minute. The Winter Garden, Broadway at 50th Street, a theater as legendary as our guest himself, who is appearing on this stage for the first time in over twenty years.

JOLSON. *(As before.)* I've been busy.

BARRY. Please give a very warm welcome to the Winter

9

Garden's most enduring bloom, the man who brought jazz to Broadway and gave the movies a voice, the World's Greatest Entertainer, the impatient Mr. Al Jolson!

(JOLSON enters.)

Song: *Swanee*

JOLSON. *(Sings.)*
I'VE BEEN AWAY FROM YOU A LONG TIME
I NEVER THOUGHT I'D MISS YOU SO
SOMEHOW I FEEL
YOUR LOVE IS REAL
NEAR YOU I LONG TO BE.
THE BIRDS ARE SINGING, IT IS SONG TIME
THE BANJOS STRUMMING SOFT & LOW
I KNOW THAT YOU
YEARN FOR ME, TOO,
SWANEE, YOU'RE CALLING ME.
OH, SWANEE, HOW I LOVE YOU, HOW I LOVE YOU,
MY DEAR OLD SWANEE
I'D GIVE THE WORLD TO BE
AMONG THE FOLKS IN D-I-X-I-EVEN KNOW MY
MAMMY'S WAITING FOR ME, PRAYING FOR ME
DOWN BY THE SWANEE
THE FOLKS UP NORTH WON'T SEE ME NO MORE
WHEN I GET TO THAT SWANEE SHORE!

SWANEE, SWANEE,
I'M GOIN' BACK TO SWANEE
MAMMY, MAMMY,
I LOVE THE OLD FOLKS AT HOME.

OH, SWANEE, HOW I LOVE YOU, HOW I LOVE YOU,
MY DEAR OLD SWANEE
I'D GIVE THE WORLD TO BE
AMONG THE FOLKS IN D-I-X-I-EVEN KNOW MY
MAMMY'S WAITING FOR ME, PRAYING FOR ME
DOWN BY THE SWANEE
THE FOLKS UP NORTH WON'T SEE ME NO MORE

WHEN I GET TO THAT SWANEE
I GET TO THAT SWANEE
I GET TO THAT SWANEE SHORE!

BARRY. Well, as my poppa used to say, Shoot me now and I'll die happy. You introduced that song in 1919, thirty years ago, and it's still news.

JOLSON. Gershwin wrote it for me. Made his reputation. Didn't hurt mine, either!

BARRY. Now let me just explain to the listeners out there that I'm speaking from my usual desk microphone, but Al has a special boom mic perched just beyond the runway that will follow him anywhere. How does it feel returning to the house where you made so much theater history?

JOLSON. Well except for that boom it looks about the same. I don't think the Shuberts have painted it since I left. Touch it up, J.J!

BARRY. Of course, one difference tonight is that you're singing on the Winter Garden stage, but you're also being listened to in Philadelphia, St. Louis, Milwaukee, Louisville, Chicago, Salt Lake City, to name a few.

JOLSON. I played all those towns. *(Shouting:)* How are ya?

BARRY. There's about 950,000 people listening right now.

JOLSON. Why, dat's close to a million, 'nless I err in my arifmetic.

BARRY. We can call it a million.

JOLSON. So how come all those folks are just sittin' home instead of going to the theater?

BARRY. Well, for the same reason that such notables as Henny Youngman, Chico Marx, and Toots Shor are here at ringside, because of a name that has guaranteed theater magic since well before World War One.

JOLSON. I thought you were gonna say Bunker Hill.

BARRY. May I mention that you're back in New York to publicize the opening of *Jolson Sings Again*, the most anticipated sequel of 1949?

JOLSON. Go right ahead.

BARRY. … *(Beat.)* People say the intense feeling you put into singing *Mammy* was your response to the loss of your mother. I don't want to step on anything too personal, but—

JOLSON. You shouldn't. She died a year after we came to America. She knew me as Asa. Poppa had left us all back in Lithuania

when he got a job as a cantor in Washington, D.C. Amerikeh! Long
way from Srednick. I hardly knew him, I was the baby. Took him four
years to save enough to send for us. Mama, my two sisters and my
brother Hirsch. We moved into a little apartment in Washington, and
then Mama got sick. I was eight.

*(A bed slides on. NAOMI lies under the blanket, very pregnant and
weak. In the Century Production JOLSON watched the next two
scenes as an observer and NAOMI and PAPA addressed an
imaginary eight to ten-year-old ASA.)*

NAOMI. Asa? Asa, where are you?

JOLSON. Right here, Mama.

NAOMI. Why don't the baby come already? I hear it screaming
inside me. You don't hear it?

JOLSON. No, Mama.

NAOMI. *Oy gevalt! Ge-VAAAAALT!* Where's my idiot husband?
Where's Moishe!!!!!!

JOLSON. He's in shul, Mama. It's shabbas today.

NAOMI. Donkey men with their donkey things. It's play for
them, making a baby. And the doctor?

JOLSON. Hirsch ran to get him. Mama, don't die. Promise you
won't ever die.

NAOMI. Never. And by me make a promise, Asa. You have a
gift of great life in you. Few have it like you do. God means you
should share it with the world. Give what you have. Give. *(He nods
assent.)* He would have killed my soul if not for you.

JOLSON. Please, Mama, please. You're scaring me.

NAOMI. Sing, my angel, my pride. Sing so you wouldn't be
scared.

JOLSON. What should I sing?

NAOMI. Welcome the shabbas angels. The angels of peace.

JOLSON. *(Sings.)*
Sholom aleichem, malachei ha-shores,
Malachei elyon,
Mi-melech malachei ha-m'lochim
Ha-kadosh baruch hu.

NAOMI. Angels! Angels! Not of peace, of death! Gevalt!

JOLSON. Mama! *(She dies.)* Mama! *(Attempting to revive her,
he sings again:)*

Sholom aleichem, malachei ha-shores,
Malachei elyon,
Mi-melech—

I kept on singing, but it didn't do no good. By the time Poppa got home, she was cold. A coupla years later, Poppa started to give me singing lessons. Only ones I ever had. He thought he could make a cantor outa me. *(Sings cantorially:)*

V'shamru b'nai yisroel es ha-shabbos,
Es ha-shabbos . . .

It's pretty but there's no kinda money in it. Now Washington is a lot busier than Srednick. Poppa's at the shul all day. Hirsch and me had no place to go but the street. There were boys from all over the place, Italy, Hungary, the Irish, and us two Litvaks, everybody mixin' it up! That's where I learned to break a nose with the first punch. But the songs they sang were great! And the colored boys, theirs were even better. I'd never seen anybody move the way they did, not in Lithuania, uh-uh! The way they danced right there on the street, people would throw money at 'em. Congressmen, sometimes! One day I figured, I can sing, let 'em throw some money at me. And they did! Lots! *(Sings.)*

SHE'S ONLY A BIRD IN A GILDED CAGE,
A BEAUTIFUL SIGHT TO SEE,
YOU MAY THINK SHE'S HAPPY AND FREE FROM CARE
SHE'S NOT, THOUGH SHE SEEMS TO BE.
'TIS SAD WHEN YOU THINK OF HER WASTED LIFE,
FOR YOUTH CANNOT MATE WITH AGE—

(A stern voice becomes booming from the upstage darkness:)

    POPPA. Asa! Asa, stop this minute! *(Light returns as he barrels downstage.) Bis meshuggeh? Bis ganz meshuggeh?* Have you lost your mind? What are you doing?
    JOLSON. Singing, poppa.
    POPPA. On the street? On the street the cantor's son sings like a vagabond? God gave you a voice to *daven* His service in shul. That's where you sing!
    JOLSON. I was just having fun!

POPPA. Four years I go without even a new suit, saving to bring you to America, so that from the congregation people should walk by and see the cantor's son singing trash *goyische* music for pennies!

JOLSON. Pennies, nothin', poppa. Congressman McKinley gave me half a dollar!

POPPA. Wise guy, smart mouth, I don't care what you got! First you bring shame on your father, then you brag what a profit you made? This is respect? From such a disgrace your mother is turning in the grave!

JOLSON. Poppa, let's go home, everybody's watching.

POPPA. Let them watch! Let them throw money while you learn a lesson! While you stay under my roof, you'll obey me. Understand? You'll obey me! Obey me!

(He starts hitting him. The hitting becomes stylized as POPPA recedes into the darkness.)

Song: *I'm Sitting on Top of the World*

JOLSON. *(Sings.)*
I'M SITTIN' ON TOP OF THE WORLD
I'M ROLLING ALONG, JUST ROLLING ALONG
AND I'M QUITTIN' THE BLUES OF THE WORLD,
I'M SINGIN' A SONG, JUST SINGIN A SONG (GLORY
    HALLELUIAH)
I JUST TOLD THE PARSON, HEY PAR, GET READY TO CALL
JUST LIKE HUMPTY DUMPTY, I'M GOIN' TO FALL
I'M SITTIN' ON TOP OF THE WORLD
I'M ROLLING ALONG, JUST ROLLING ALONG

(He returns to the table, where BARRY is waiting.)

BARRY. That was terrific, Jolie, just terrific. A great song.

JOLSON. You ain't heard nothin' yet.

BARRY. So take us forward, how'd you get into vaudeville?

JOLSON. It was actually my brother's idea. We started going to vaudeville theaters as soon as we could get in, and some of the acts in those days were pretty low grade. So Hirsch said, "We can do better than that, why don't we put an act together?" A few jokes, a coupla songs, and we were out of the house, touring in vaudeville.

BARRY. A cantor's son? Your father didn't mind?

JOLSON. Nah, he was proud of me. He always loved everything I did. He was a scholar, my father, a rabbinical sort of a figure. But he was a sharp dealer when he had to be. I once sent him a coat, very beautiful, and when he called to thank me, he asked how much it cost. Well, it cost a couple hundred or more but I didn't want him to know, so I said thirty bucks. The next day he called again and said, "Send me eight more, I sold it for forty."

BARRY. But that's a long time after your vaudeville years. What happened to Hirsch?

JOLSON. Well, first he changed his name to Harry, and Asa Yoelson became Al Jolson.

BARRY. Isn't it also around this time that you first put on blackface?

JOLSON. That's right, 1904, in Philadelphia. Lots of acts did it in those days. I wasn't even twenty. Harry wrote a sketch with me as a comic porter. Right away I killed 'em. The makeup loosened me up somehow. Turned me into a star.

BARRY. So it became your act?

JOLSON. *(Walking into the special. Music —* The Little Victrola *under.)* I love my brother. Harry's my best audience. I send money home regular. He had a pretty voice, Harry, still does, but I was the hit of the act and he decided, well, he decided he might look better on his own.

(A shabby dressing room slides on.)

HARRY. Asa, lemme ask you something. Do me a favor and stop hamming it up behind my back.

JOLSON. When do I ham it up?

HARRY. When don't ya? I got one solo number in this act and I'd like for the audience to be lookin' at me while I sing it.

JOLSON. Maybe you should try singin' it with more pep.

HARRY. Maybe you should stop mugging during my number.

JOLSON. I'm just tryin' to help you get laughs.

HARRY. Laughs? *The Orphan's Dying Prayer* ain't supposed to get laughs.

JOLSON. Why not?

HARRY. Why not? Why not? It's a sad song!

JOLSON. Not the way you do it.

HARRY. What's wrong with the way I do it?

JOLSON. For one thing, you just stand there like a stick. It's boring.

HARRY. It's boring to you because it's not your number.

JOLSON. It's boring to the audience. Ever look at their faces? You put 'em to sleep.

HARRY. You cocky little punk, you wouldn't have an act without me. For two cents I'd walk out on you this minute.

JOLSON. *(Slamming a coin on the table.)* Keep the change.

(Out on stage into the song.)

Song: *The Little Victrola*

JOLSON. *(Sings.)*
I KNOW A COUPLE IN FULL DRESS AND GOWN
WHO USED TO GO TO THE PARTIES IN TOWN
BUT HE GOT JEALOUS
OF ALL OF THE FELLAS
SHE LOOKED SO PRETTY THEY KEPT CROWDING AROUND!
    HARRY.
HE SAID, WITH ENVY I'LL TURN 'EM ALL GREEN
HE WENT AND BOUGHT HER A VICTOR MACHINE
    JOLSON.
WITH THAT VICTROLA HOME
    HARRY.
THEY NEVER HAVE TO ROAM
    BOTH.
CAUSE HE GETS HER ALL ALONE
THEN THEY START THE VICTROLA
THE LITTLE VICTROLA
AND UP COMES THE RUG FROM THE FLOOR
AT NO MORE PARTIES ARE THEY TO BE FOUND
HE LIKES TO HAVE HER WHERE NO ONE'S AROUND
THAT'S WHY HE BOUGHT THE VICTROLA
THE LITTLE VICTROLA
THEY NEVER GO OUT ANY MORE
AND AFTER DANCING SHE'S ALL OUT OF BREATH
HE LIKES TO TAKE HER AND HUG HER TO DEATH
THEN THEY START THE VICTROLA
THE LITTLE VICTROLA
AND GO DANCING AROUND THE FLOOR

HARRY.

SOMETIMES HE DOESN'T ROLL HOME UNTIL THREE,

JOLSON.

SHE SITS UP WAITING, AS MAD AS CAN BE

THEN GRABS HIS COLLAR

AND STARTS IN TO HOLLER

BOTH.

"GUESS YOU'RE FORGETTING THAT YOU'RE NO LONGER FREE!"

JOLSON.

SHE SAYS, "NOW DEARIE, YOU'RE WASTING YOUR LIES

CUT OUT THAT INNOCENT LOOK IN YOUR EYES"

HARRY.

HE TRIES TO INTRODUCE

MANY A LAME EXCUSE,

BOTH.

THEN THEY BOTH SAY WHAT'S THE USE?

THEN THEY START THE VICTROLA

THE LITTLE VICTROLA

AND UP COMES THE RUG FROM THE FLOOR

AT NO MORE PARTIES ARE THEY TO BE FOUND

JOLSON.

NO MORE PARTIES! NO MORE PARTIES!

BOTH.

HE LIKES TO HAVE HER WHERE NO ONE'S AROUND

THAT'S WHY HE BOUGHT THE VICTROLA

THE LITTLE VICTROLA

THEY NEVER GO OUT ANY MORE

JOLSON.

MORE … MORE … MORE … MORE *(Holds note.)*

HARRY.

AND AFTER DANCING SHE'S ALL OUT OF BREATH

HE LIKES TO TAKE HER AND HUG HER TO DEATH

(HARRY squeezes JOLSON tight to make him stop the note.)

BOTH.

THEN THEY START THE VICTROLA

THE LITTLE VICTROLA

AND GO DANCING AROUND,

DANCING AROUND,

GO DANCING AROUND THE FLOOR.

(Back in the dressing room:)

JOLSON. You sang the high note again. That's my note!

HARRY. What, it's got your name on it?

JOLSON. Might as well have. You do the harmony under.

HARRY. You're just jealous because Florence Goodgarden said my voice was that much prettier than yours.

JOLSON. Florence Goodgarden has buck teeth and a squint.

HARRY. And she's not the only one. Everybody says it.

JOLSON. Who else?

HARRY. Louise Driscoll and Gracie DeFleur and Clara Cunningham.

JOLSON. So what if they did? A pretty voice ain't worth two bits if you don't know how to sell it.

HARRY. Go to hell.

JOLSON. And I know something you don't about Clara Cunningham.

HARRY. Such as?

JOLSON. She has a funny kind of bellybutton. Like the wrong end of a balloon.

HARRY. You saw her bellybutton?

JOLSON. More than saw.

HARRY. You're a liar.

JOLSON. Oh yeah? Well if I'm lyin', it's her I'm lyin' with.

HARRY. You shtupped Clara Cunningham? *(JOLSON nods.)* Well, little brother, the joke's on you. You told me you'd never shtup a Jewish girl.

JOLSON. Clara Cunningham?

HARRY. Her real name is Sadie Shapiro. You said shtupping a Jewish girl would be like spitting on Mama's grave. Ha ha. *(JOLSON lunges at HARRY and they fight.)* Stop it, Asa, Asa! I was only kidding. Jeez! I was kidding.

JOLSON. You ever make that kind of a joke again I'll kill you. I mean it. Schmuck. And don't call me Asa.

(HARRY takes the coin and exits.)

JOLSON. So each of us went out as a single. I was almost twenty and it was my luck to hit San Francisco right after the earthquake. I was just what they needed. They couldn't clap enough. You know I don't like to brag, but after one week I was the most famous man in the city. Well, Caruso had left the week before. After two weeks there were so many Jolson imitators they started holding competitions. I blacked up and entered one, incon-jeeto. Took third place. Some guy in the back kept yelling, Get offa there, ya bum, you stink! Today that man is a network executive. Around that time I married wife Number One. We were just kids. It was a mistake. A mistake I kept on making, till finally I got it right. I toured the West Coast and Rocky Mountain states for months. I wowed 'em everywhere. Los Angeles in 1908. It's changed. And then I got invited to join up with Lew Dockstader's Minstrels.

(Underscore: Camptown Races. *He walks into the special:)*

JOLSON. Dockstader was the king of minstrel shows back then. He played only the first-class theaters. I was sure he was my ticket to New York. I learned a lot from Dockstader. He rehearsed like a maniac. The troupe was famous for precision, fancy tambourine work. He had seventy guys to drill, all in blackface. We put on a great show, and I had the only solo spot besides Dockstader's. But I wanted more. Not more money. Not even more solos. More ... more ....

(DOCKSTADER glides on.)

DOCKSTADER. More what?

JOLSON. More life in the music, Mr. Dockstader.

DOCKSTADER. Jolson, what are you talking about? We're a hit every place we go. The public loves you.

JOLSON. But the music isn't ....

DOCKSTADER. Isn't what?

JOLSON. What if they've had enough Stephen Foster and all that stuff left over from the Civil War? It's the twentieth century!

DOCKSTADER. Where were you born, Jolson?

JOLSON. Lithuania.

DOCKSTADER. I can't hear you.

JOLSON. Lithuania.

DOCKSTADER. Where the hell is that?

JOLSON. It's part of Russia.

DOCKSTADER. Part of Russia! And you're telling me about the Civil War, and defiling the memory of Stephen Foster, the greatest composer America has ever produced?

JOLSON. I didn't mean to defile his memory.

DOCKSTADER. *Jeanie with the Light Brown Hair* and *Camptown Races* are jewels in the crown of American music.

JOLSON. Maybe once in a while we could change hats. Those songs are pretty but they're tired. The colored people don't sing them any more, if they ever did. As long as we're in blackface, why don't we sing black?

DOCKSTADER. I get it. This is about New Orleans again. Now I'm sorry we ever played there.

JOLSON. Why? That colored music is wonderful. The way they sing and play, it's like they were davening.

DOCKSTADER. What's davening?

JOLSON. It's what my poppa does in the synagogue. It's wailing with devotion.

DOCKSTADER. Your poppa in the synagogue and a bunch of hopped-up nigs on junkweed? Jolson, you need a vacation.

JOLSON. It makes you wanna dance, even when you're tired.

DOCKSTADER. No, Jolson, what it makes you want to do is fuck (hump). That jazz music you like so much is about one thing, and one thing only. Intercourse. Sex.

JOLSON. Nothing wrong with that.

DOCKSTADER. There's everything wrong with it! We play a family trade, and gyrations below the waist are not wanted. Music that encourages lascivious thoughts is not wanted.

JOLSON. Even in blackface?

DOCKSTADER. Especially in blackface. The American public does not wish to contemplate a whole subnation of coons making babies.

JOLSON. You think it's that different from white people?

DOCKSTADER. If you were really white you wouldn't ask that question.

JOLSON. Mr. Dockstader, last week a man in the hotel dining room called me a kike and I broke his nose. What you just said would be insulting if I thought there was something better about being white. Then I might get mad and break your nose. And what would happen then to your soggy rendition of *Jeanie with the Light Brown Hair*? Somebody might get up and sing it as if Jeanie was the kind of girl who actually liked gyrations below the waist, and then where would we be? No sir, Mr. Dockstader, it wouldn't do, and so with your kind permission I'll go back to the hotel and pack my bags and get the next train outa here to someplace where I can give what I have to give, even if it's jazz.

DOCKSTADER. You're under contract, Jolson. Quit me and you'll be finished with minstrel work.

JOLSON. I sure as shit hope so. *(DOCKSTADER exits. Walking into the special.)* That had to be the dumbest move I ever made. But I was right. People loved the new music and I gave it to 'em with both barrels. I sang like no white guy ever did before, and I ended up on this very stage. The Shubert brothers opened the Winter Garden on March the 20th, 1911. My very first night on Broadway, they stood for my curtain call. There's a rumor that I threw the script away that night. But that didn't happen—not for another coupla years. By then I was Name Above the Title. I didn't exactly throw the script away. I just sorta made it ... optional. *(Emoting as GUS:)* "You see, Colonel Fitzwallawalla, it wasn't Miss Amanda's doin' at all. It was me dat clumb up in de tree in disguise and threw dem rotten apples at Master Marmaduke. Miss Amanda was on de veranda de whole time, writin' dat secret love letter, which I delibbered by accidemp to de Grand Dook." *(To audience.)* Can you follow this? Not me. Listen folks, forget about the plot, let Jolie sing you some songs. Okay, cast dismissed, Ricky, gimme some house lights, I wanna see who came. Here's a new one. Heard it just the other day, and it made me think of you. Professor, pass the mustard.

Song: *You Made Me Love You*

JOLSON, *(Sings.)*
YOU MADE ME LOVE YOU
I DIDN'T WANNA DO IT
I DIDN'T WANNA DO IT
YOU MADE ME WANT YOU
AND ALL THE TIME YOU KNEW IT
I GUESS YOU ALWAYS KNEW IT
YOU MADE ME HAPPY SOMETIMES
YOU MADE ME GLAD

(Speaks.) I remember that weekend.

BUT THERE WERE TIMES, DEAR,
YOU MADE ME FEEL SO BAD.

YOU MADE ME SIGH FOR

(I DIDN'T WANNA TELL YOU
I DIDN'T WANNA TELL YOU)
SOME LOVE FROM YOU THAT'S TRUE
YES, I DO, 'DEED I DO, Y'KNOW I DO,
GIVE ME GIVE ME WHAT I CRY FOR
YOU KNOW YOU GOT THE BRAND OF KISSES THAT I DIE FOR
YOU KNOW YOU MADE ME LOVE YOU

YOU MADE ME SIGH FOR
I DIDN'T WANNA TELL YOU
I DIDN'T WANNA TELL YOU
SOME LOVE FROM YOU THAT'S TRUE
YES, I DO, 'DEED I DO, Y'KNOW I DO,
GIVE ME GIVE ME WHAT I CRY FOR
YOU KNOW YOU GOT THE BRAND OF KISSES THAT I DIE FOR
YOU KNOW YOU MADE ME LOVE YOU

*(JOLIE's dressing room slides on. He trades his jacket for an ornate
dressing gown and towels his face. A buxom blonde in a skimpy
wrap appears at the door.)*

MAE. Jolie, mind if I come in?

JOLSON. Come in, Mae. You ain't dressed much.

MAE. You ain't either.

JOLSON. Yeah. but it's my room.

MAE. That's awright, it's my body.

JOLSON. Sure is. I was watchin' ya from the wings tonight.

MAE. Yes you were.

JOLSON. Jolie don't lie, baby. Keep movin' like that, you'll be
promoted outa the chorus in no time.

MAE. Yes I will.

JOLSON. Glad I'm not onstage, with you shimmyin' behind my
back.

MAE. I'd never upstage you, Jolie. I'd never even try.

JOLSON. Wouldn't ya?

MAE. Course not. Everybody knows how you had them trained
elephants fired on accounta the audience liking 'em too much.

JOLSON. I like you, Mae. Where ya from?

MAE. Brooklyn. You?

JOLSON. Lithuania. Know where that is?

MAE. Ain't it halfway to Siberia?

JOLSON. I guess it is. We came this way instead. My mama brought us over. *(Moving toward her.)* I miss my mama.

MAE. Course you do. You sing about her enough.

JOLSON. You got yours?

MAE. Never had a mother. Some jerk took advantage of my aunt. Mind? *(Dipping into the blackface jar and dabbing her nose— later removed with a towel.)* What's it like wearin' this stuff?

JOLSON. I love it.

MAE. Pretending you're an eight-ball, what the hell for?

JOLSON. It lets me get away with stuff I couldn't do with a naked *punnim*. I'd scare 'em too much.

MAE. Whaddaya mean?

JOLSON. Listen, Mae. An audience is a tiger you gotta learn how to tame. They wanna love ya. They've come from all over the place, uptown, downtown, who the hell knows what kinda day they've had? But when you step onto that stage, every heartbeat they have is yours. You gotta respect that. If I was big and wild and free like I am, but lookin' like a white man, they'd run for the door. Snappin' my fingers and wigglin' my ass, singin' that eight-ball rhythm, and cryin' for my mama, as a white man? A Litvak yid? It's un-American.

MAE. Ever heard the blues, Jolie?

JOLSON. Sure.

MAE. I'm gonna sing the blues, and I won't black up to do it.

JOLSON. Ha!

MAE. I ain't kiddin'. I'm gonna be exactly who I am, exactly the woman I am. I'm gonna sing with everything a woman's got, and I won't black up.

JOLSON. They'll throw ya in the clink.

MAE. Jails don't scare me. I'm a big girl.

JOLSON. So I see.

MAE. You know what jail is? *(Indicating the blackface.)* This.

JOLSON. You're wrong. That's freedom. I slap it on, and I'm not a Litvak any more. I'se one o' de children of Israel, slavin' fo' de Pharaoh, jus lak de Bible say. And mah song is mah redemption, yeah!

MAE. You're a live one, Jolie. Bet you could teach a girl a lot.

JOLSON. No one better, baby. *(MAE removes his robe.)* Why don't I come up some time and see ya? *(On the verge of a kiss, JOLSON breaks away and returns to BARRY'S table. MAE and the dressing room vanish.)* There were a lot of bonuses to being the World's Greatest Entertainer. Me, a kid from the streets, getting invited to the White House for breakfast.

BARRY. Who was President?

JOLSON. George Washington. No, I breakfasted with every President from Woodrow Wilson on. And Truman got me bagels. That reminds me of another story. Back around 1918 they invited me to be a founding member of the Westchester Biltmore Country Club. I played golf there for years, and if the policy changed nobody told me about it until some time in the twenties when I brought my friend Harry Richman up to play a round. The management takes me into a side office and says, "We're very sorry, Mr. Jolson, but Mr. Richman can't play here." I go, "Why not" and they say, "We're sorry but Jews are not permitted." So I tell them, "He's only half Jewish, can he just play nine holes?" And then I quit.

BARRY. Wasn't it also in 1918 that you sang at the Met? The first time any popular music was sung from that stage.

JOLSON. It was a war bond benefit. I followed Caruso. In fact he was still getting his "Ridi Pagliacci" applause when I stuck my head through the curtain and said, "You ain't heard nothin' yet." And Caruso loved it. He was a street kid, too.

BARRY. You had a lot of famous fans, didn't you?

JOLSON. Presidents, prizefighters, bootleggers. I had to start adding extra performances on Sunday nights so the stars of the other Broadway shows could see me. Not only the stars. The gypsies. Everybody.

(JOLSON crosses to runway.)

Song: *Where Did Robinson Crusoe Go with Friday on Saturday Night?*

JOLSON. *(Sings.)*
OVER A THOUSAND YEARS OR MAYBE MORE,
OUT ON AN ISLAND ON A LONELY SHORE
ROBINSON CRUSOE LANDED ONE FINE DAY,
NO RENT TO PAY,
NO WIFE TO OBEY.
HIS GOOD MAN FRIDAY WAS HIS ONLY FRIEND
HE DIDN'T BORROW OR LEND,
THEY BUILT A LITTLE HUT,
LIVED THERE TILL FRIDAY BUT

SATURDAY NIGHT IT WAS SHUT.
OH WHERE DID ROBINSON CRUSOE GO
WITH FRIDAY ON SATURDAY NIGHT?
EVERY SATURDAY NIGHT THEY WOULD START IN TO ROAM
AND ON SUNDAY MORNING
THEY'D COME STAGGERING HOME
THEY WENT HUNTING FOR RABBITS
WHEN THE WEATHER GREW COLDER
BUT CRUSOE CAME HOME WITH A HAIR ON HIS SHOULDER
OH WHERE DID ROBINSON CRUSOE GO
WITH FRIDAY ON SATURDAY NIGHT?
WHERE DID ROBINSON CRUSOE GO
WITH FRIDAY ON SATURDAY NIGHT?
WHEN THE SUN WOULD GO DOWN
AND THE SKY WOULD GROW DARK
WOULD THEY TAKE EACH OTHER FOR A WALK IN THE
    PARK?
ON THIS ISLAND WERE WILD MEN, AND CANNIBALS
    SWIMMIN'
AND YOU KNOW WHERE THERE ARE WILD MEN
THERE MUST BE WILD WOMEN
OH WHERE DID ROBINSON CRUSOE GO
WITH FRIDAY ON SATURDAY NIGHT?

*(JOLSON's dressing room slides on. This time he changes into a
    smoking jacket. A knock at the door.)*

JOLSON. If it's flowers leave 'em outside. If it's money, slip it
under the door.

ETHEL. *(Outside the door.)* Neither one, Mr. Jolson. I'm sorry,
maybe I should leave you alone?

JOLSON. Hey, who've we got out there? Sounds like an angel.

ETHEL. My name's Ethel. Ethel Delmar. I'm a friend of Polly
Swanson's. She got me backstage and I figured as long as I was here I
could meet you and tell you how wonderful you are, Mr. Jolson.

JOLSON. *(Escorting her in.)* Call me Jolie. Come in, Ethel. You
a dancer, too?

ETHEL. Yeah, that's right. I'm with the *Scandals*. Sure love to
be in a first-class show like yours, Mr. Jols–I mean, Jolie.

JOLSON. Aren't you too pretty for the chorus?

ETHEL. I don't know. Am I?

JOLSON. You asking me or the mirror?

ETHEL. This is such a beautiful dressing room. Much bigger than Eddie Cantor's.

JOLSON. You see the show tonight?

ETHEL. Actually, I've seen it a few times. I come whenever you do a Sunday night special for the show folks. Never thought I'd get up the moxie to say hello to the World's Greatest Entertainer. Would it be okay if I have a little drink to settle my nerves?

JOLSON. As long as you're not a Fed, try some of Joe Kennedy's latest batch, over there.

ETHEL. *(Hiking her dress up and taking a flask from her garter.)* It's okay, I got my own. Bottoms up.

(She drains the flask.)

JOLSON. Let's hope so.

ETHEL. Aren't you a naughty little pup! And me just out of the convent. You're swell, Jolie. Let me tell you a secret. When you're onstage, it feels like you're singing right to me. Honest to God. You just make me melt.

JOLSON. You look pretty solid to me, baby.

ETHEL. I got soft spots all over. You just gotta know where to press.

JOLSON. Who's naughty now?

ETHEL. "Not I," said the little red hen.

JOLSON. So what are you doing tonight?

ETHEL. It's pretty late. I thought I'd say my prayers and go to bed.

JOLSON. What about saying your prayers at the Cotton Club and saving bed for later?

ETHEL. Ooh, Jolie, that sounds like fun! I just gotta dump Polly. We had something lined up, but I can get out of it.

JOLSON. I thought you said you were just gonna say your prayers.

ETHEL. Maybe my prayers have been answered.

JOLSON. You don't miss a beat, do you?

ETHEL. I'm a dancer, remember? My body's just full of rhythm and jazz. Aw, but my poor little flask is empty.

JOLSON. There's hooch in the car. Let's get uptown.

ETHEL. There's just one thing. Are you gonna marry me?

JOLSON. Marry you? Do de word "premature" ring a bell?

ETHEL. I don't mean tonight.

JOLSON. That's a relief.

ETHEL. But a girl likes to know where she stands. Suppose I fall for you, even more than I have.

(She kisses him hard.)

JOLSON. Wow, baby! They teach you that in the convent?

ETHEL. You'd never be bored with me in the house.

JOLSON. Ethel, you know what my wife said when she divorced me? I was a wonderful lover and a lousy husband.

ETHEL. Better than the other way round.

JOLSON. You like high times, crowds, parties, all that stuff?

ETHEL. Sure. When do we start?

JOLSON. You mean we haven't already? Tell Polly you'll see her later. I'll have the car brought up in five minutes.

(He slaps her tush.)

ETHEL. Toodle-oo, Jolie.

(She slaps his tush and goes.)

JOLSON. Toodle-oo to you. *(He steps into the special as the set slides off.)* Wife Number Two. Actually, it was bigamy. I married her and a bottle at the same time. She ended up liking the bottle better than me. They're still together after all these years. At least, I think they are. Her and me don't chat much. *(The stage goes dim. ETHEL is sitting alone in an institutional chair.)* Ethel, they told me you were in here. *(No response.)* Hey, sweetie, it's Jolie. I come to see you.

ETHEL. Jolie. I thought you forgot where they sent me.

JOLSON. You know I've been on the road for four months.

ETHEL. The road, the road, where a man can fuck (screw) like a toad. I need a drink.

JOLSON. Ethel—

ETHEL. Whatsa matter, laugh-man, can't you take a joke?!!!

JOLSON. *(Beat.)* Is there anything you need, do you want anything? *(No response.)* The grounds are pretty, don't you think? Trees and flowers and everything. Ethel?

ETHEL. Are we divorced yet?

JOLSON. Honey!

ETHEL. Is it final yet?

JOLSON. Yes.

ETHEL. So that's it then, huh. Now you've told me, I guess you don't have to bother coming out here anymore.

JOLSON. C'mon, Ethel. I'd marry you again in a second if you just lay off the booze.

ETHEL. Marry you again! That's a good one! You think I miss getting clobbered that much?

JOLSON. Quit it, will ya? I smacked you one time when you were loaded.

ETHEL. Oh sure, and it really helped me stop drinking, didn't it?

JOLSON. I'm sorry.

ETHEL. Marry you again? Sure, why not? Let's do it right here in the psycho ward underneath one of them Jew canopies. Bottoms up!

JOLSON. That's enough, goddammit! It's not a psycho ward, Ethel. It's a very fine hospital.

ETHEL. Kiss my ass.

JOLSON. That's nice talk.

ETHEL. Yeah, well, I'd hate to get emotional or anything.

JOLSON. I'll see you in a couple weeks.

ETHEL. Don't bother.

(Lights change. He crosses back to the table with BARRY.)

BARRY. And then you went to California and made motion picture history. Just how did that come about?

JOLSON. What?

BARRY. *The Jazz Singer.* Everything okay?

JOLSON. Yeah, sure. *The Jazz Singer* started out as a play based on my life although Georgie Jessel actually played the part on Broadway. *(JOLSON holds his nose.)* 1926 it was. I'd been the Shubert's top star for about a dozen years, playing nonstop on Broadway and the road, nonstop. I was—almost forty, and I was getting worn out. When Warner Brothers called me about making *Jazz Singer* as a talking picture, I was very interested.

BARRY. And they paid you in Warner Brothers stock?

JOLSON. No performer had ever had a deal like that before. And when the picture became a world sensation, I was bigger than ever.

BARRY. So you moved to Hollywood to make more pictures.
JOLSON. I liked the climate.

Song: *California Here I Come*

JOLSON. *(Sings.)*
WHEN THE WINTRY WINDS ARE BLOWING
AND THE SNOW IS STARTING IN TO FALL
THEN MY EYES TURN WESTWARD, KNOWING
THAT'S THE PLACE THAT I LOVE BEST OF ALL.
CALIFORNIA, I'VE BEEN BLUE
SINCE I WENT AWAY FROM YOU
I CAN'T WAIT TILL I GET GOING
EVEN NOW I'M STARTING IN TO CALL:

CALIFORNIA, HERE I COME,
RIGHT BACK WHERE I STARTED FROM
WHERE BOWERS OF FLOWERS
BLOOM IN THE SPRING
EACH MORNING AT DAWNING
BIRDIES SING AND EVERYTHING
A SUN-KISSED MISS SAID "DON'T BE LATE,"
THAT'S WHY I CAN HARDLY WAIT
OPEN UP THAT GOLDEN GATE
CALIFORNIA, HERE I COME!

CALIFORNIA, HERE I COME,
RIGHT BACK WHERE I STARTED FROM
WHERE BOWERS OF FLOWERS
BLOOM IN THE SPRING
EACH MORNING AT DAWNING
BIRDIES SING AND EVERYTHING
A SUN-KISSED MISS SAID "DON'T BE LATE,"
THAT'S WHY I CAN HARDLY WAIT
OPEN UP THAT GOLDEN GATE
CALIFORNIA, HERE I COME!

(Lights change. JOLSON and JOSEPHINE DUNN meet.)

JOLSON. Hiya, Josephine. You're looking lovely as usual.

JOSEPHINE. Good morning, Al. Thank you.

JOLSON. Aw, c'mon, Josie.

JOSEPHINE. All right, Jolie, but don't call me Josie.

JOLSON. How ya think it's going so far, baby?

JOSEPHINE. I have great confidence in Lloyd.

JOLSON. Didja ever make a picture with him before?

JOSEPHINE. Not since sound came in.

JOLSON. You think it's here to stay?

JOSEPHINE. Well, *The Jazz Singer* is a big enough hit.

JOLSON. Thanks to me.

JOSEPHINE. Yes, of course. Jolie.

(LLOYD BACON comes in, a droll and tweedy Englishman.)

LLOYD. Good morning, everyone. Shall we have a go?

JOLSON. Good morning, Lloyd.

JOSEPHINE. *(Overlapping.)* Good morning, Lloyd.

LLOYD. *(Walking onto the runway.)* Let's try the camera here for now. Shall we rehearse a bit? Ready? Action!

JOLSON. *(Overacting isn't even the word:)* Molly! Molly, where are you going?

JOSEPHINE. Away from you. Yes, it's true. Don't look at me like that.

(They both do a take out to the camera simultaneously.)

JOLSON. But you know how I feel about ya, Baby. Gosh, I thought you were that way about me, too. Haven't I given you everything in the world? Fine clothes, diamonds, a darling little baby and my love.

JOSEPHINE. Your love? That's a laugh! I never loved you, you sap. I used you to become a star! Now I'm leaving. I've already sent Sonny ahead.

JOLSON. Oh, please, Molly. I've got to see my Sonny again. Lemme see him. Haven't I been good to you, Molly? I've gone broke paying for your extravagances and never said a word about it.

JOSEPHINE. Let's not get into a gabfest at this hour of the night. You can meet him in the park tomorrow morning.

LLOYD. Cut! Lovely, Josephine, just right. Jolie, old boy, I think you might tone it down a bit.

JOLSON. Like how exactly?

LLOYD. Well, you see, with the camera we're in much closer than the back row of an opera house.

JOLSON. It's kinda strange not having an audience to tell me how I'm doing.

LLOYD. I'll tell you, Jolie. That's why I'm here.

JOSEPHINE. I'm having a smoke.

(She withdraws.)

JOLSON. So? How'm I doing?

LLOYD. The night club scenes are fine, Jolie. You have such endearing pep. But these more intimate scenes don't require so much movement. Try not to roll your eyes so much when you look at the camera. In fact, try not to look at the camera. Try to just miss it. Let's have another bash. Josephine!

JOSEPHINE. All set.

LLOYD. Aaaaaand, Action!

JOLSON. Molly! Molly, where are you going?

JOSEPHINE. Away from you. Yes, it's true. Don't look at me like that.

JOLSON. But you know how I feel about ya, Baby. Gosh, I thought you were that way about me, too. Haven't I given you everything in the world?

LLOYD. Cut! Jolie, give me half of that. Give me less than half.

JOLSON. You want me to get a measuring cup?

JOSEPHINE. About that smoke.

(She withdraws.)

LLOYD. Just act naturally, Jolie.

JOLSON. When I act natural you tell me it's no opera house. Do you know I'm the highest paid performer in the history of Broadway? The entire history of Broadway.

LLOYD. And how do you wish me to assimilate this information?

JOLSON. I know audiences and I know what works, that's all. *The Jazz Singer* is driving 'em crazy all over the world.

LLOYD. That is certainly true, and *The Singing Fool* will be ten times as great if you just allow yourself to be directed.

JOLSON. How come you don't give Josephine no direction for a change?

LLOYD. Josephine, darling. Let's take another crack at the old scene, shall we? And this time, why don't you try smoking during the first few lines?

JOSEPHINE. That's a great idea, Lloyd. I wish I'd thought of it.

LLOYD. Aaaaaand, Action!

JOLSON. Molly! Molly, where are you going?

JOSEPHINE. Away from you. *(Blowing smoke in his face.)* Yes, it's true. Don't look at me like that.

JOLSON. *(Gagging and furious.)* But you know how I feel about ya, Baby. Gosh, I thought you were that way about me, too. Haven't I given you everything in the world? Fine clothes, diamonds, a darling little baby—

LLOYD. Cut! Jolie, watch the eye popping.

JOLSON. Well, she's looking at me like I just farted or something.

JOSEPHINE. I'll thank you to remember, Mr. Jolson, that I am a lady. That is the most vulgar remark I have ever heard. I'm afraid I really must lie down. Call me when you're ready for a take.

(She goes.)

LLOYD. Jolie, I'm going to adjust the lighting. In the next setup we shoot the song. Why don't you have a look at the bedroom set? Think about your lost little boy. Try to make him real.

(As LLOYD speaks a child's bed rolls on. LLOYD exits. JOLSON picks up and fondles a stuffed animal. He sinks onto the bed.)

Song: *Sonny Boy*

JOLSON. *(Sings.)*
CLIMB UPON MY KNEE, SONNY BOY,
YOU ARE ONLY THREE, SONNY BOY
YOU'VE NO WAY OF KNOWING
THERE'S NO WAY OF SHOWING
WHAT YOU MEAN TO ME, SONNY BOY.
WHEN THERE ARE GREY SKIES
I DON'T MIND THE GREY SKIES
YOU MAKE 'EM BLUE, SONNY BOY
FRIENDS MAY FORSAKE ME
LET 'EM ALL FORSAKE ME

I'LL STILL HAVE YOU, SONNY BOY.
YOU CAME FROM HEAVEN
AND I KNOW YOUR WORTH
YOU'VE MADE A HEAVEN
FOR ME RIGHT HERE ON EARTH.
WHEN I'M OLD AND GREY, DEAR
PROMISE YOU WON'T STRAY, DEAR
I LOVE YOU SO, SONNY BOY.
YOU'RE SENT FROM HEAVEN
AND I KNOW YOUR WORTH
YOU'VE MADE A HEAVEN
FOR ME RIGHT HERE ON EARTH.
WHEN I'M OLD AND GRAY, DEAR,
PROMISE YOU WON'T STRAY, DEAR,
I LOVE YOU SO, SONNY BOY.

(He goes back to the table.)

BARRY. Your most successful song commercially.

JOLSON. Corny as a deuce, but it bought me a house in Palm Beach.

BARRY. And yet your next few pictures had nothing like the success of the first two.

JOLSON. You mean, they stank.

BARRY. Well, I wouldn't—

JOLSON. They stank! The scripts were awful and the Brothers Warner gave me lousy budgets. I didn't care. I was too busy setting up house in the Valley.

BARRY. With your beautiful young bride, Ruby Keeler.

JOLSON. She was dancing in a show the first time I saw her. I brought her out to the coast, set her up with a job and married her. She was nineteen. I was forty-three. It was pure marital bliss.

(RUBY enters. He crosses to meet her.)

RUBY. Hey baby. Like the new dress?

JOLSON. What are you doin' home, Ruby? Ain't ya at the club tonight?

RUBY. Yeah, but I wanted to talk to you first. I'll make it there in time.

JOLSON. Gimme a kiss. *(She does.)* Baby, I love that dress, but if you're late it makes me look bad. I put my name on the line for you, Ruby....

RUBY. *(Fondling him.)* I know, honey, but you're so busy shootin' the movie and you got me dancin' at the club almost every night.

JOLSON. You wanted a job, didn't ya'? It's the best club in town.

RUBY. You got a call today from Jack Warner. They're puttin' together a live show featurin' all the musical talent. It's some kinda benefit....

JOLSON. A live audience, huh. Top billing?

RUBY. You ever get anything else?

JOLSON. That's poppa's girl.

RUBY. So how's about lettin' baby do a number with poppa?

JOLSON. I don't do doubles. You know that, Ruby.

RUBY. They want you to do a whole bunch of stuff. Just one little number with me. You said you wanted to help me, sweetie...

JOLSON. I got you the job in the club....

RUBY. I want people to know I'm your wife. I want them to see us perform together.

JOLSON. Well, why not?

RUBY. Ya mean it?!!! Oh, sweetie, I promise I'll make you so proud of me!

JOLSON. I am already. Okay, let's try somethin'. Sing with me. . .

RUBY. What about the club?

JOLSON. Don't worry about it. I'll give 'em a call.

Song: *Red Red Robin* (Part I)

JOLSON. *(Sings.)*
WHEN THE RED RED ROBIN COMES BOB BOB BOBBIN'
ALONG, ALONG
    TOGETHER.
THERE'LL BE NO MORE SOBBIN' WHEN HE STARTS
    THROBBIN'
HIS OLD SWEET SONG
    JOLSON.
WAKE UP, WAKE UP YOU SLEEPY HEAD
    RUBY.
GET UP, GET UP, GET OUT OF BED

TOGETHER.
CHEER UP, CHEER UP, THE SUN IS RED
LIVE, LOVE, LAUGH AND BE HAPPY!
   RUBY.
WHAT IF I'VE BEEN BLUE, NOW I'M WALKIN' THROUGH
FIELDS OF FLOWERS
   TOGETHER.
RAIN MAY GLISTEN BUT STILL I LISTEN
FOR HOURS AND HOURS
I'M JUST A KID AGAIN, DOIN' WHAT I DID AGAIN
SINGING A SONG
WHEN THE RED RED ROBIN COMES BOB BOB BOBBIN'
   ALONG!

   JOLSON. Now I do this little step here. Try it. *(She does.)* That's good, but don't look at your feet. It's not professional.
   RUBY. How'm I supposed to learn?
   JOLSON. Look at my feet.

(Lights change—several years have passed.)

   RUBY. Hey, sweetie, instead of that step we always do, what about this?

(Elaborate tap break.)

   JOLSON. Where'd you get that?
   RUBY. Jimmy taught it to me.
   JOLSON. That's Cagney, I suppose?
   RUBY. Yeah, we do it in the new picture, on the counter of a bar.
   JOLSON. Everything he does reeks of the saloon. Not for me.
   RUBY. C'mon, sweetie, just try it. It ain't that hard.
   JOLSON. If it ain't that hard, how come you gotta look at your feet?
   RUBY. I'm sorry. It's a bad habit.
   JOLSON. You're pickin' up a lot of bad habits.
   RUBY. What's that supposed to mean?
   JOLSON. Nothin'. It's just … sometimes I wonder if you're the same girl I married.
   RUBY. Sure I am. Why wouldn't I be?
   JOLSON. Now that you're a big shot movie star. Going to

parties without me.

RUBY. Like when?

JOLSON. Like the one Dick Powell threw at the beach.

RUBY. You said you were too tired.

JOLSON. You coulda stayed home with me.

RUBY. He's my co-star. It was job duty.

JOLSON. Sure, with a bunch of sweaty young guys in bathing suits.

RUBY. Jolie, you're jealous. That's so sweet. *(Kisses him.)* Half those boys are nancies, anyway.

JOLSON. What about the other half? I don't like the way them guys look at you.

RUBY. It's nothing. Plenty of girls used to look at you the same way.

JOLSON. Used to?!!!

RUBY. And still do. Joan Blondell thinks you're the bee's knees.

JOLSON. She does?

RUBY. Sure. And so do I. Now let's not fight over nothing. Come on and practice this step with me.

(He tries without success.)

JOLSON. I can't do that. It ain't my style. Let's just stick with what we know, okay?

RUBY. Okay.

Song: *Red Red Robin* (Part II)

JOLSON. *(Sings.)*
WHEN THE RED RED ROBIN COMES BOB BOB BOBBIN'
ALONG, ALONG
   TOGETHER.
THERE'LL BE NO MORE SOBBIN' WHEN HE STARTS
   THROBBIN'
HIS OLD SWEET SONG
   JOLSON.
WAKE UP, WAKE UP YOU SLEEPY HEAD
   RUBY.
GET UP, GET UP, GET OUT OF BED

TOGETHER.
CHEER UP, CHEER UP, THE SUN IS RED
LIVE, LOVE, LAUGH AND BE HAPPY!

(Lights shift—More years pass.)

RUBY. I don't know about this song, Jolie. Let's do something from *Go into Your Dance*. That's what people want to see, not this tired old number.

JOLSON. If they wrote me any good numbers in that picture, I'd sing 'em.

RUBY. Us, darling. They want us to do a number together to promote the picture at the Hollywood Bowl show. Why can't we do one of our numbers?

JOLSON. I did that movie as a favor to Warners. We're not a team, Ruby.

RUBY. Oh, I'm sorry, I thought I was in the movie with you, Al. My mistake.

JOLSON. Now don't get snotty. You were fine in the picture, I just don't want 'em thinkin' we're gonna make a habit of co-starring.

RUBY. *Go into Your Dance* made more money than your last three pictures combined.

JOLSON. Here it comes! So now you de jockey, is that it, Miss Big Shot *Forty-Second Street*?

RUBY. You could give me a little credit, that's all.

JOLSON. You get enough credit, baby. You think I don't know what they're all sayin' about you bein' so hot and me bein' washed up?

RUBY. Who says that?

JOLSON. Everybody. I know they do. I walk into the commissary and I see it all over their fuckin' (goddamn) faces.

RUBY. You know I hate that word! Jolie, you've said yourself you've got more money than you could spend in three lifetimes. What do you care about some stupid Hollywood gossip?

JOLSON. Then it is true. I knew it.

RUBY. I hate it when you get like this. There's just no talking to you.

JOLSON. I'm sorry, kid. We'll drop it. Let's go to the track.

RUBY. I told you, I'm not going to the track with you any more.

JOLSON. Oh, come on, on account of one little punch?

RUBY. One little punch? Giving Walter Winchell a black eye is not what I call a little punch.

JOLSON. I didn't like what he wrote about you.

RUBY. But I didn't sock him, did I? You know how mortified I was? I could have died right then and there.

JOLSON. Forget it! Come on, fish-ears, General Pershing's running at Santa Anita.

RUBY. No! *(Beat.)* You go. I've got a golf date at three.

JOLSON. With who?

RUBY. Some friends.

JOLSON. You didn't say nothing about no golf date. Who with?

RUBY. Friends. Dick Powell.

JOLSON. I'm not invited?

RUBY. You won't play with me ever since when I beat you at Hillcrest.

JOLSON. Why Dick Powell? That shtunk, what are you up to with him?

RUBY. Up to? He happens to be my leading man.

JOLSON. Some leading man!

RUBY. He's a great leading man!

JOLSON. Sure, if ya like toothpaste.

RUBY. Toothpaste!!?? What are you talking about?

JOLSON. I'm your leading man, and don't you forget it!

RUBY. You don't want to be my leading man, you just said so!

JOLSON. Don't tell me what I said, I know what I fucking said! (I know what I goddamn said!)

RUBY. You don't know anything, you're a maniac!

JOLSON. Everyone in this business is a maniac. You have to be! Try to do something beautiful in this world and for every one that appreciates you there's ten that resent you. You can't even count on the audience any more with all the competition from goddamn radio and movies. Audiences today got the memory of a three-year-old. I worked with some of the biggest names on Broadway and in vaudeville and where are they now? Forgotten. I was a star when you were still in diapers, and I'll be a star when you and Dick Powell are demonstrating putters in Macy's fucking (goddamn) window.

RUBY. What do you want? Right this minute, what do you want?

JOLSON. I don't know!... I want you to rehearse with me. Go over the number.

RUBY. The old one? *(He nods.)* Okay, let's get it over with.

Song: *Red Red Robin* (Part III)

JOLSON. *(Sings.)*
WHEN THE RED RED ROBIN COMES BOB BOB BOBBIN'
ALONG, ALONG
> **TOGETHER.**

THERE'LL BE NO MORE SOBBIN' WHEN HE STARTS
> THROBBIN'

HIS OLD SWEET SONG
> **JOLSON.**

WAKE UP, WAKE UP YOU SLEEPY HEAD
> **RUBY.**

GET UP, GET UP, GET OUT OF BED
> **TOGETHER.**

CHEER UP, CHEER UP, THE SUN IS RED
LIVE, LOVE, LAUGH AND BE HAPPY!
> **RUBY.**

WHAT IF I'VE BEEN BLUE, NOW I'M WALKIN' THROUGH
FIELDS OF FLOWERS
> **TOGETHER.**

RAIN MAY GLISTEN BUT STILL I LISTEN
FOR HOURS AND HOURS
I'M JUST A KID AGAIN, DOIN' WHAT I DID AGAIN
SINGING A SONG
WHEN THE RED RED ROBIN COMES BOB BOB BOBBIN'
> ALONG!

(They sing the song to its conclusion, RUBY improvising tap breaks all over the place. Lights change. JOLIE is at a dressing room table.)

STAGE MANAGER. *(Offstage.)* Fifteen minutes, Mr. Jolson. Fifteen minutes, Miss Keeler.

JOLSON. Herb, Ruby still ain't here. Whyncha see if she's outside signing autographs?

RUBY. *(Entering, with a large envelope.)* Here I am. Don't flip your wig.

JOLSON. Where the hell ya been? We're on in fifteen.

RUBY. I'm not going on.

JOLSON. What are you talking about?

RUBY. It would be a bad idea.

JOLSON. You're nervous, kid. Been puttin' out for the cameras too long. Don't worry. I'll carry you, like always.

RUBY. Well, I just can't tell you how reassuring that is, but even so I'm not going on.

JOLSON. Don't be stupid, Ruby. You know how important this benefit is. Everybody in Hollywood will get to see you in a classic Jolson number with Jolie, and you think it's a bad idea.

RUBY. Everybody in Hollywood can see me at the movies. Which is more than you can say.

JOLSON. That Garland kid would jump at the chance and she's got more star power than you'll ever have.

RUBY. Stop it, Al. Just stop it.

JOLSON. Stop what? Get dressed, will ya?

RUBY. I'm not in a star contest with Judy Garland! You may think you have to compete with the whole world but I was raised different. My people taught me that love matters.

JOLSON. Yeah, love mattered so much to your shanty Irish mother she made me fork over a million bucks before we could get married.

RUBY. Leave my mother out of this! I didn't want your feckin' (blamin') money. I make more than you do now, anyway.

JOLSON. We'll see how long that lasts.

RUBY. Who cares? I'm not in a star contest with you, either! I know damn well I'm just an ordinary girl who's had a lot of lucky breaks. Eleanor Powell dances better, Alice Faye sings better and Katie Hepburn sure as hell acts better and she's a lot prettier, too. So what? I know how to have fun when I'm offstage and you don't. You're a selfish, insecure, bad-tempered, coarse old man whose best days are so long gone not even God could revive them.

JOLSON. Where the fuck (hell) do you get off talking to me like that? I'm not old.

RUBY. Deaf, that's what you are!

JOLSON. You watch what happens when I step out on that stage tonight. It'll be my show! Mine! Crosby, Nelson Eddy, Don Ameche! I'll wipe 'em off the bill. I fart better than Don Ameche sings! You think I'm gonna roll over and let these Hollywood shmucks turn me into just another day player! All I need is my audience.

RUBY. That's all you'll get.

JOLSON. You're so full of shit (crap) you must have gone to an outhouse with a ladle.

RUBY. Al, I'm tired. Tired of your feckin' (blamin') insults and your feckin' (blamin') ego and your feckin' (blamin') childish tantrums.

JOLSON. And I'm tired of that stupid word. What the fuck is Feck? Feck! Why can't you say fuck like a mensch instead of talkin' like some shanty Irish scrubwoman? (And I'm tired of that stupid word. Blamin'! What the hell is that? Why can't you cuss like a mensch instead of talkin' like some shanty Irish scrubwoman?)

RUBY. You really want to know, Jolie Baby? I'll tell you. It's because the man I've been fecking is a gentleman and he don't like me to say fuck. (It's because the man I'm screwin' is a gentleman and he don't like me to talk like a tramp.)

JOLSON. Wh–what man is that?

RUBY. His name is John. I met him playing golf. He's in real estate and he's awfully sweet and he's even my own age. Think of that! *(Gives him the envelope.)* Everything's drawn up right here. You consent to an incompatibility decree and we'll keep the rest out of the papers.

JOLSON. This is a joke. You're kiddin', right? You bitch.

(He swings, she dodges.)

RUBY. I loved you once, I think. When I was too young to know better. But you're a mean man, and John is a kind one. He makes me happy. You'd have killed my soul if it wasn't for him.

JOLSON. What did you say?

RUBY. Goodbye, Al.

JOLSON. No, you can't go. No! What about the number? Ruby, I need ya.

RUBY. No, you don't. You're the world's greatest entertainer. Go get 'em.

STAGE MANAGER. *(Offstage.)* Five minutes, Mr. Jolson. Five minutes, Miss Keeler.

RUBY. *(As she exits.)* Herb, tell Eddie there's a change. Jolie's doing a single.

(JOLSON sits before the "mirror" and with demonic concentration gets into full blackface, first outlining the "lips," filling in the face, pulling on white gloves and, finally, the wig.)

JOLSON. Hello, Asa. Think they'll know it's you?

Song: *My Mammy*

JOLSON. *(Sings.)*
EVERYTHING SEEMS LOVELY WHEN YOU START TO ROAM
THE BIRDS ARE SINGING THE DAY THAT YOU STRAY
BUT WAIT UNTIL YOU ARE FURTHER AWAY;
THINGS WON'T LOOK SO LOVELY WHEN YOU'RE ALL
    ALONE
HERE'S WHAT YOU'LL KEEP SAYING
WHEN YOU'RE FAR FROM HOME:
MAMMY, MAMMY,
THE SUNS SHINES EAST, THE SUN SHINES WEST
BUT I KNOW WHERE THE SUN SHINES BEST
MAMMY, MAMMY,
MY HEART STRINGS ARE TANGLED AROUND ALABAMMY.
I'M A-COMIN', I'M SORRY IF I MADE YOU WAIT
I'M A-COMIN', I HOPE AND PRAY THAT I'M NOT LATE
MAMMY, MAMMY,
I'D WALK A MILLION MILES
FOR ONE OF YOUR SMILES
MY MAMMY!
MAMMY, MY LITTLE MAMMY,
THE SUNS SHINES EAST, THE SUN SHINES WEST
BUT I KNOW, I KNOW WHERE THE SUN SHINES BEST
IT'S MAMMY I'M TALKIN' ABOUT, NOBODY ELSE'S!
MY HEART STRINGS ARE TANGLED AROUND ALABAMMY.
I'M A-COMIN', I'M SORRY IF I MADE YOU WAIT
I'M A-COMIN', I HOPE AND PRAY THAT I'M NOT LATE
MAMMY, LOOK AT ME! DONCHA KNOW ME?
I'M YOUR LITTLE BABY
I'D WALK A MILLION MILES
FOR ONE OF YOUR SMILES
MY MAMMY!

END OF ACT ONE

ACT II

Song: *Toot Toot Tootsie*

JOLSON. *(Sings.)*
YESTERDAY I HEARD A LOVER SIGH
GOODBYE, OH ME OH MY,
SEVEN TIMES HE GOT ABOARD HIS TRAIN
AND SEVEN TIMES HE HURRIED BACK
TO KISS HIS LOVE AGAIN
AND TELL HER:
TOOT TOOT TOOTSIE, GOODBYE
TOOT TOOT TOOTSIE, DON'T CRY
THAT CHOO-CHOO TRAIN THAT TAKES ME
AWAY FROM YOU, YOU'LL NEVER KNOW
HOW SAD IT MAKES ME
KISS ME TOOTSIE, AND THEN
DO IT OVER AGAIN
WATCH FOR THE MAIL
I'LL NEVER FAIL
IF YOU DON'T GET A LETTER
THEN YOU'LL KNOW I'M IN JAIL
TOOT TOOT TOOTSIE, DON'T CRY
TOOT TOOT TOOTSIE, GOODBYE!

(Dance break.)

WATCH FOR THE MAIL
I'LL NEVER FAIL
IF YOU DON'T GET A LETTER
THEN YOU'LL KNOW *(Spoken.)* I'M ILLITERATE
TOOT TOOT TOOTSIE, DON'T CRY
TOOT TOOT TOOTSIE, GOODBYE!

BARRY. I'm exhausted watching you.

JOLSON. I'm exhausted being me.

BARRY. There are people who've followed your career from the beginning who think your voice sounds better today than it ever did.

JOLSON. They're just glad they haven't lost their hearing.

BARRY. Is it hereditary or do you vocalize every day?

JOLSON. Well I got my poppa's pipes, for sure. But don't forget I had a nice long rest, called the Thirties.

BARRY. Go on, you were still active then.

JOLSON. Radio-active. And some bit parts in movies.

BARRY. You stole every one of them.

JOLSON. Thanks, Barry, but remember, you can only steal what isn't yours. I didn't work near as much, or as hard, as I did in the Twenties. Let's face it, I wasn't a kid any more. Like Sophie Tucker says, on radio nobody has liver spots.

BARRY. You came back to Broadway with a hit.

JOLSON. My last one, 1940. *Hold On to Your Hats.* But I pushed too hard. Couple months into the run I went to the hospital with pneumonia. I looked into the eyes of the Grim Reaper, and he said, "Go back to radio." But I couldn't stand it. The singing was okay, but I hated reading off a script and the cuckoos upstairs wouldn't let me improvise. They were afraid I'd run overtime and squeeze out the commercials. In my day we sold tickets, not soap.

(MARTHA enters with microphone on a stand which she places center.)

MARTHA. *(Handing him a script.)* Here's the latest changes, Mr. Jolson. Chuck's up there.

JOLSON. Listen, kid, call me Jolie and I'll try to remember your name.

MARTHA. It's Martha. Can I bring you some coffee?

JOLSON. Black, thanks. *(She goes. He fumbles for reading glasses.)* Are we taking it from after the song, Chuckie?

CHUCK'S VOICE. *(On speaker.)* Right, Jolie. Aaaaand, cue.

JOLSON. Good evening, ladies and gentlemen, and welcome to the Colgate-Palmolive Parade of Stars. Jolie's got a great show for you tonight—Chuckie, what's that squiggle after "tonight"?

CHUCK. A semi-colon.

JOLSON. Oh my, aren't we grand! My guests include Paramount's rising young star Bob Hope, the very lovely and talented Miss Deanna Durbin, Harry Parkyakarkus, Tony Martin, and the comedy team of Seymour and DuLess. And I've got more talent in my little finger than all of 'em put together. I'm not gonna say that, I just had to get it off my chest.

CHUCK. Jolie, we're timing this.

JOLSON. *(Racing:)* Not-to-mention-the-orchestra-under-Gordon-Jenkins-and-the-Louis-Silvers-Malibu-Sextet....

CHUCK. Jolie, we air at seven tonight. Stop messing around. Again from the top. Aaaaand, cue!

JOLSON. *(Sticking out his tongue.)* Good evening, ladies and gentlemen, and welcome to the Colgate-Palmolive Parade of Stars. Jolie's got a great show for you tonight—*(Low voice.)* Semi-colon. *(Out loud.)* I got a full colon myself.

CHUCK. Jolie!

JOLSON. My guests include Paramount's rising young star Bob Hope, the very lovely and talented Miss Deanna Durbin, Harry Parkyakarkus, Tony Martin, and the comedy team of Seymour and DuLess. There will also be a live wrestling match between the Knights of Columbus and the B'nai Brith.

CHUCK. Jolie!

JOLSON. That's funny, why don't I say it?

CHUCK. It will offend people.

JOLSON. Oh, come on, anybody who's offended by that deserves to be.

CHUCK. Jolie, we air at seven! Martha will write it down and we'll talk about it next week.

JOLSON. If I stick with this script, we'll be off the air next week.

CHUCK. Jolie, this rehearsal is costing 4500 dollars a minute! The time for script discussion is over. You may be the World's Greatest Entertainer, but you'll read what's on the goddamn page.

JOLSON. I don't like being told off, Chuck. Especially over a squawkbox. Step down here and talk to me.

CHUCK. We don't have time for this.

JOLSON. Time? What do you know about time? You been directing for what? Six months? *(Pulling out his bankbook.)* This is how much I've made in this business, putz! What have you got?

CHUCK. I've got friends.

JOLSON. *(Beat.)* Better hope they can find you a new job.

(JOLSON gives CHUCK the finger, walks to chair and sits. MARTHA brings him coffee.)

MARTHA. Jolie, here's your coffee.

JOLSON. Thanks, honey.

MARTHA. I thought it was funny. About the Knights of Columbus, I mean. My dad's one.

JOLSON. That's sweet of you, Martha. Aren't you too pretty to be a script girl?

MARTHA. Stop it, Jolie, you'll make me blush.

JOLSON. No, really. You're a mouse's ear, know what I mean? You should be on camera. You know I own a big chunk of Warner Brothers. Come here.

MARTHA. That's all right, Mr. Jolson. I have work to do.

JOLSON. *(Taking her hand.)* I think we're on hold while Chuckie schmoozes the cuckoos. Wouldn't ya like to be in pictures?

MARTHA. I don't think my boyfriend would approve.

JOLSON. You got a boyfriend, huh? At your age? What's his name?

MARTHA. Warren. He's in the Navy. On the *Arizona*. I'm flying out to Hawaii next week to see him.

JOLSON. Well if you haven't seen him in a while, you might enjoy a little warm-up.

MARTHA. I don't think a man as old as you are should talk this way to a girl like me.

JOLSON. I'm only thinking you might like some practice.

MARTHA. I don't need practice! I'm in love!

(She goes.)

Song: *Hello Central, Give Me No Man's Land*

JOLSON. *(Sings.)*
WHEN THE GREY SHADOWS CREEP
AND THE WORLD IS ASLEEP
IN THE STILL OF THE NIGHT
BABY CLIMBS DOWN A FLIGHT
FIRST SHE LOOKS ALL AROUND
WITHOUT MAKING A SOUND
THEN BABY TODDLES UP TO THE TELEPHONE
AND WHISPERS IN A BABY TONE:
HELLO, CENTRAL, GIVE ME NO MAN'S LAND
MY DADDY'S THERE

MY MAMA TOLD ME
SHE TIPTOED OFF TO BED
AFTER MY PRAYERS WERE SAID
DON'T RING WHEN YOU GET THE NUMBER
OR YOU'LL DISTURB MAMA'S SLUMBER
I'M AFRAID TO STAND HERE AT THE PHONE
CAUSE I'M ALONE
SO WON'T YOU HURRY!
I WANNA KNOW WHY MAMA STARTS TO WEEP
WHEN I SAY NOW I LAY ME DOWN TO SLEEP
HELLO, CENTRAL, GIVE ME NO MAN'S LAND!

I'M AFRAID TO STAND HERE AT THE PHONE
CAUSE I'M ALONE
SO WON'T YOU HURRY!
I WANNA KNOW WHY MAMA STARTS TO WEEP
WHEN I SAY NOW I LAY ME DOWN TO SLEEP
HELLO, CENTRAL, GIVE ME NO MAN'S LAND!

(Lights rise on COLONEL WEBSTER'S War Department Office. WEBSTER is on the phone.)

WEBSTER. But, sir, General Patton's HQ has already green-lighted the Morale Project. I have clearance as of 0900 tomorrow. Yessir, I appreciate the guidance, but—No, I know what you mean, sir—Entertainers are going to be difficult to manage in the military arena.

JOLSON. *(Entering.)* Excuse me, are you Colonel Webster?

WEBSTER. I'll be right with you. *(To phone.)* I have had plenty of experience organizing large-scale events, sir. I did the New Year's Eve Gala—Yeah, we had Charlie McCarthy!

JOLSON. The young lady said go right in.

WEBSTER. *(To the phone.)* Just a moment, sir— *(To JOLSON.)* I'm very sorry, sir, but I have an appointment coming in at ten and I can't speak with you right now.

JOLSON. But your secretary—

WEBSTER. Look, Mr.—

JOLSON. Jolson.

WEBSTER. Mr. Jolson! Oh my god! I'm sorry, sir, I didn't recognize you in person.

JOLSON. You and everybody else.

WEBSTER. Please sit down, Mr. Jolson. *(To phone.)* He's here. Yes, Sir, of course I will. Margaret, yes— "all my love, Jolie"—Got it, sir. *(Hangs up.)* Mr. Jolson, I apologize for keeping you waiting. You're early.

JOLSON. Well, I'd like to get started.

WEBSTER. General Bradford asked me to relay his admiration and ask for your autograph for his wife Margaret.

JOLSON. Thank the General and it would be my pleasure. Now about the Service Show.

WEBSTER. Can I just say, Mr. Jolson, my mother never stops playing your records. She'll faint when she hears we're working together.

JOLSON. Maybe you should break it to her slow. Colonel, you're my final gateway to this project, am I right? I've been shoveling a lot of bureaucratic malarkey from politicians and Pentagon brass. I don't know why, it seems pretty cut and dried to me; bunch of soldiers—entertainment. Where's the big problem?

WEBSTER. None, hopefully. It's my assignment to work with you on devising a feasible way to bring entertainment to the troops.

JOLSON. I thought we'd call the operation "Service Stars."

WEBSTER. We can't do that.

JOLSON. Why not?

WEBSTER. First of all, we tend to use initials and SS ....

JOLSON. Right, we'll leave Hitler out of the deal. How about "Broadway on the Battlefield"?

WEBSTER. We're calling it the United Services Organization.

JOLSON. Catchy.

WEBSTER. The USO. We plan to try and enlist many of the top stage and screen stars to perform for the boys. You're the first.

JOLSON. Now you're talking! So the way I got it figured, you fly over me, a conductor and the orchestra—

WEBSTER. Orchestra! How many guys are in an orchestra?

JOLSON. Usually around thirty.

WEBSTER. Thirty!

JOLSON. Twenty.

WEBSTER. That's not possible.

JOLSON. A band.

WEBSTER. We gotta keep it small.

JOLSON. Combo?

WEBSTER. I doubt it.

JOLSON. Colonel, I don't play the ukulele.

WEBSTER. The General was thinking a piano player.

JOLSON. And that's it?

WEBSTER. I don't really have much of a budget for this.

JOLSON. I'll pay my own way, Colonel Webster.

WEBSTER. We were kind of counting on that. We hoped you'd start by doing a show at the training camp in Alaska and then back stateside to North Carolina....

JOLSON. Whoa, Trigger! I spoke with President Roosevelt about going to the front.

WEBSTER. Mr. Jolson, I don't think that's feasible.

JOLSON. Unless I read the wrong newspapers, that's where the troops are.

WEBSTER. It would be very dangerous to transport entertainers to the front. General Bradford suggested some of the state-side training camps.

JOLSON. Those boys can go to the movies!

WEBSTER. We have enough trouble just getting the Red Cross to the front, Mr. Jolson, let alone a bunch of entertainers....

JOLSON. All right, all right, forget the front, but I'm not playing the back. How about the side? How close can you get me?

WEBSTER. Well, something tells me we want to keep you away from General MacArthur.

JOLSON. Colonel, all I know about war comes from the movies, but I do know that over there there's a lot of scared young kids far from everyone they care about. Afraid they'll never see their mothers or sweethearts again. I just want to show them that somebody back here cares about them enough to go over and make 'em smile.

WEBSTER. We'll do the best we can. How does North Africa strike you?

JOLSON. I'll bring my suntan lotion. *(With a light change, JOLSON dons a combat jacket and addresses the audience.)* Thanks, fellas. Thanks a lot. I wanna sing you a song I first sang in World War One, maybe some of your folks heard me then. And I wanna dedicate it to the friend of a friend, a sailor named Warren who went down with the *Arizona* at Pearl Harbor. But first I have to tell you that the stage I'm standing on was built this morning by a couple of colored platoons, and they've got 'em sitting all the way in the back there. I think that stinks, don't you? I'm on stage because of them. You fellas come right down here. Come on! Right down front. Thank you. Thank you. Your people and my people both know that when life gets hard we can turn it into a song. And from the song we get the strength to fight on. Professor....

Song: *Rock-a-Bye Your Baby with a Dixie Melody*

JOLSON. *(Sings.)*
MAMMY MINE
YOUR LITTLE ROLLIN' STONE THAT ROLLED AWAY,
STROLLED AWAY.
MAMMY MINE
YOUR ROLLIN' STONE IS ROLLIN' HOME TODAY,
HERE TO STAY.
JUST TO SEE YOUR SMILIN' FACE
SMILE A WELCOME SIGN,
WHEN I'M IN YOUR WARM EMBRACE
LISTEN, MAMMY MINE:
ROCK-A-BYE YOUR BABY WITH A DIXIE MELODY
WHEN YOU CROON, CROON A TUNE
FROM THE HEART OF DIXIE.
JUST HANG MY CRADLE, MAMMY MINE,
RIGHT ON THAT MASON-DIXON LINE
AND SWING IT FROM VIRGINIA
TO TENNESSEE WITH ALL THE SOUL THAT'S IN YA,
"WEEP NO MORE, MY LADY," SING THAT SONG AGAIN FOR
ME
AND "OLD BLACK JOE" JUST AS THOUGH
YOU HAD ME ON YOUR KNEE.
A MILLION BABY KISSES I'LL DELIVER
IF YOU WOULD ONLY SING THAT "SWANEE RIVER,"
ROCK-A-BYE YOUR ROCK-A-BYE BABY WITH A DIXIE
    MELODY.

"WEEP NO MORE, MY LADY," SING THAT SONG AGAIN FOR
    ME
AND "OLD BLACK JOE" JUST AS THOUGH
YOU HAD ME ON YOUR KNEE.
A MILLION BABY KISSES I'LL DELIVER
IF YOU WOULD ONLY SING THAT "SWANEE RIVER,"
ROCK-A-BYE YOUR ROCK-A-BYE BABY WITH A DIXIE
    MELODY.

(Back to table with BARRY.)

BARRY. That song would make you homesick for Dixie even if you're from Hoboken. How many stops on that USO tour?

JOLSON. Alaska, London, in Algiers I met Ike, then Tunisia, and Sicily right after the landing. Then I got real sick and they sent me home where it turned out to be some kinda African malaria. Once I was back on my feet, the USO said Europe would be too strenuous so they let me tour the service hospitals here, the Purple Heart Circuit. And dat's where my angel come to me!

BARRY. Would that have been in Hot Springs, Arkansas?

JOLSON. A town sweeter than honey, my friend, where first I laid eyes on Miss Erle Chennault Galbraith, a young woman of distinguished family and dazzling charm. She was an X-ray technician in the hospital where I was playing, and she stood out in that audience like an orchid in a bowl of walnuts. Of course, I needed to know if she was as pretty close up as she looked from the stage.

(ERLE appears on an elegant chair, talking on a white phone. She and JOLSON speak the next line together, adjust the pronouns.)

ERLE & JOLIE. And then right there on the spot he/I asked me/her if I/she wanted to get into pictures.

(ERLE continues alone as JOLSON and BARRY vanish. She has a marked Arkansas drawl.)

ERLE. Daddy, I haven't a clue how old he is—Well I don't know how old you are, and I don't care to. What difference does it make? Mr. Jolson has been thoroughly businesslike in every way—Certainly not, and I wouldn't let him if he did try! Daddy!—Well, I never thought of being an actress, but it might be fun. Worth a try, huh?—What accent? Daddy, maybe it won't amount to more than a lovely vacation, so what? I'll stay with the Clarendons and Cousin Clarisse will be my chaperone. Oh Daddy, think of all the lovely clothes I'll find in Beverly Hills. Don't you want your little girl to look pretty? *(Lights dim and rise; time has passed.)*

Oh, Daddy, it's been the most wonderful day! Jolie took me to the races and we met Bing Crosby and Rita Hayworth! And Jolie won $13,000 in the first race!—Yes, she is just as gorgeous in real life— No, I haven't started another picture—How many times have you seen it?—Daddy, I told you, in the second shot of the harem scene, I'm the one on the left in the veil with the dark sequins—Well, I hope my next part is bigger, too, but it doesn't matter all that much. Because I'm having such a marvelous time. The weather is beautiful and the people are all so healthy-looking and Jolie is a laugh a minute—Yes, Cousin Clarisse laughs, too. She just adores Jolie!— I'm not sure, but I'll probably come home for a week or two around Thanksgiving. Jolie's going out on another hospital tour, and I want to show you and momma all the clothes he's bought me. He has wonderful taste—Oh now, Daddy, don't be such a putz... It's a word Jolie taught me... It means a little so-and-so. Yes, I love you. And Momma, too. I'll see you real soon! *(Lights dim and rise; more time has passed.)*

Daddy, I am so sorry I had to leave without a proper goodbye, but the minute the hospital called I jumped on a flight to Los Angeles. Yes, pneumonia. It's very bad. They're removing part of his lung today. Well, for a man his age it could be very—yes, now I do. Fifty-eight. *(Losing it.)* Daddy, if anything happens to him, I'll just—! Yes, Daddy. Yes—Momma's prayers, too? I'll tell him.

(She hangs up and exits. JOLSON's hospital bed slides on. He is getting an IV drip.)

    ERLE. *(Entering with a handbag and flowers.)* Jolie, darlin'? It's me.
    JOLSON. Erle! You're my first visitor. How do I look?
    ERLE. Like you need some flowers.

(She starts to put them in a vase.)

    JOLSON. The only flower I need is you.
    ERLE. If you can be that corny, I know you're on the mend.
    JOLSON. Have you talked to the doctor?
    ERLE. He said the remainder of your lung looks healthy.
    JOLSON. Did he leave me enough to sing with? Maybe they'll bronze the rest.
    ERLE. You are the silliest man.
    JOLSON. I've always been a cut-up, but this is ridiculous. Did he say if I could sing again?
    ERLE. Jolie darlin', for now you just need to get your strength back. I brought you some good nourishing broth.

JOLSON. Is there a prettier nurse anywhere in this world?

ERLE. I'm sure there's several, but I'm the one you're stuck with.

JOLSON. Marry me, Erle. You could be a rich widow very soon.

ERLE. That's a new kind of proposal. Are you on painkillers?

JOLSON. I don't know what I'm on. If I could get outa this bed I'd go down on one knee, but everybody's seen me do dat already. Erle, listen, I'm crazy about you and I don't want that to go to waste. What are you, twenty-one? You have so much life ahead of you. I could be part of it.

ERLE. More than part. Much more.

JOLSON. You mean it?

ERLE. Yes.

JOLSON. Yes you mean it, or yes you'll marry me?

ERLE. You'll have to ask my father. But I'll twirl him round my finger whatever he says to you. Jolie, you have given my life its happiest hours, and I accept your proposal with all my heart.

JOLSON. Oh, baby, lemme hear that again! Oh, baby, I'm so happy!

(He tries to get up and coughs.)

ERLE. Jolie, take it easy! Don't make me a widow before we're even married.

JOLSON. There's something you should know. I'm very sturdy in the love department but I shoot blanks. Can't give you any children.

ERLE. I'm glad you told me. I hadn't thought about children.

JOLSON. You wanna change your mind?

ERLE. Jolie! I'm in love with you. In sickness and in health, for richer, for poorer....

JOLSON. That part we don't have to worry about.

ERLE. I just wonder why you didn't ask me sooner.

JOLSON. Well, you know I got it wrong a few times. The way I feel about you, I don't want to make any dumb mistakes.

ERLE. I love you too much to let you, don't worry. Do we want a more romantic setting for our first kiss?

JOLSON. Just let 'em take my blood pressure first.

(They kiss and slide off as HARRY COHN'S poolside furniture slides on. COHN is on the phone.)

COHN. Look buddy, I don't just produce movies, I make hits. It'll sell. Trust me. *Yankee Doodle Dandy* made a fortune! You like the idea but what? A different star? Who but Jolson was ever as big as Cohan? Who? Fuck him, he's dead! (Screw him, he's dead!) You think Jolson's not marketable anymore? Look, I know music and those Jolson tunes are classics. We could string them together with Mickey Mouse's life and sell tickets. Very funny. I think he's under contract with Disney. Jolson's on his way now and I'll sell him on it. I don't need to suck up. I kiss the feet of that kind of talent. Sure, I'm making him a producer. I'll tell you why. I dealt with him when I was starting out, years ago. Yeah, I was a music promoter, you know pushing songs. He treated me the way he treats everybody, like shit (crap). He'd keep me waiting outside the Winter Garden stage door for hours, and I promised myself that one day I'd have the sonofabitch working for me!

JOLSON. *(Offstage.)* Harry, the butler pinched me.

HARRY. He's here. My ass itches already. *(Hangs up. JOLSON enters.)* Jolie my friend, it's a *mechaya* to see you looking so good.

JOLSON. This is a surprise, I'm supposed to look like crap.

COHN. On Oscar night I should look so good.

JOLSON. Little Harry Cohn, no more hanging around stage doors, huh?

COHN. You old horse thief.

JOLSON. Speaking of which, let's get to business, I don't want to miss the Prefecta.

COHN. Right to the point, huh?

JOLSON. *Nu, vod den?*

COHN. Okay, Columbia is ready to produce a picture based on your life.

JOLSON. I'm sorry. I'm a little hard of hearing in my old age and I thought you said you wanted to do a picture of my life.

COHN. *Yankee Doodle Dandy* was a blockbuster and I think you have a lot more fans than George M. Cohan ever did.

JOLSON. You don't have to convince me, Harry. I think I'm fascinating. I would need a nice percentage of the gross.

COHN. The profits.

JOLSON. Fifteen.

COHN. Ten.

BOTH TOGETHER. Twelve and a half.

(They shake hands.)

JOLSON. What about Ethel? Jesus, what about Ruby? Harry, my life ain't been no musical comedy.

COHN. This won't be a documentary, Jolie. It's Hollywood.

JOLSON. I've got some more requirements.

COHN. Shoot.

JOLSON. Script approval.

COHN. Fine.

JOLSON. We soft pedal Ruby and those first wives of mine.

COHN. Hell, we could combine them into one broad.

JOLSON. Good idea. Casting approval.

COHN. You can even pick the actor who plays you.

JOLSON. The actor who plays ... I'm gonna play me, Harry.

COHN. Jolie, what are you saying? We're going to start with vaudeville. No one'll believe you're twenty.

JOLSON. Why not?

COHN. Cause there ain't enough gauze from here to Pasadena.

JOLSON. I play me or forget the whole thing.

COHN. C'mon, Jolie. It's your life. It's your music. It's your picture.

JOLSON. Then let it be me on screen.

COHN. Out of the question.

JOLSON. I need to audition to play myself? *(Goes down on one knee and sings.)*

I'D WALK A MILLION MILES
FOR ONE OF YOUR SMILES
MY MAAAAMY–

(He has a hard time getting up.)

COHN. Jolie, you sound great, but it just took you 200 frames to get off your knee there. We gotta keep the film under three hours. We'll get an unknown to play you. That won't take the audience away from your story. We have a contract player named Larry Parks who's a real dynamo.

JOLSON. What about the singing?

COHN. Suppose Parks lip-synchs and we dub your voice.

JOLSON. Lip-synchs?

COHN. Nobody sings live any more, Jolie. They all dub themselves. So why not dub somebody else?

JOLSON. Then you gotta pay me to record the songs.

COHN. Five grand.

JOLSON. Fifteen.

BOTH TOGETHER. Ten.

(They shake hands.)

JOLSON. And if the movie's a hit we release an album of the sound track.

COHN. That might work.

JOLSON. Might work! It's brilliant! When do we start shooting?

COHN. Yesterday.

(They shake.

ERLE is at a table setting out a tea service and cake. JOLSON comes storming in.)

ERLE. Jolie! What are you doing home?

JOLSON. They kicked me off the set.

ERLE. Why?

JOLSON. The director said I was holding up production. And that *mamzer* Harry Cohn let him do it. That sonofabitch was a song-plugger thirty years ago, a nobody, a fucking (a goddamn) nothing!

ERLE. I'll set a place for you.

(She goes out.)

JOLSON. And what was I doing? Trying to get some more life into that *ferkakte* Parks. He dances like an ox on stilts. All my life I've only had one step, but nobody else can do it.

(ERLE returns with another setting and a glass of bourbon as well.)

ERLE. Here's something a little stronger while the tea steeps.

JOLSON. Thanks, baby. Goddammit, it's my life they're fucking with! (screwin' with!)

ERLE. Jolie, please, you know how I hate harsh language. Stop pacing and sit down to tea with me. I made Momma's butterscotch spice cake.

JOLSON. I died and went to heaven the day I married you.

(He sits.)

ERLE. Now just for ten minutes I want you to forget how big a star you are and save all your twinklin' for me. Forget about Harry Cohn and Columbia Pictures and Larry Parks and the whole silly gang.

JOLSON. I can't believe those fuckin' bastards (sons of bitches) threw me off the set.

ERLE. *(Pouring tea.)* Jolie, you know I don't like to dwell on our differences, but where swearing is concerned, I will never approve. That's one side of my upbringin' I just won't curb.

JOLSON. Oh come on, baby, words can't hurt ya.

ERLE. I'm sorry, darlin', but you know I feel very strongly about it. You never spoke like that when we were courting! If you continue to swear in my presence, I'll have to resort to drastic measures.

JOLSON. Sweetie pie, there's not a drastic bone in your beautiful body.

ERLE. Thank you, Jolie, but many ladies in the South are familiar with the method employed by Mrs. Mark Twain.

JOLSON. Wha... if her husband uttered a wicked word?

ERLE. That's right. Sugar?

JOLSON. Mm. What would Mrs. Twain do?

ERLE. Every time he swore she would say, excuse me, "Eat shit, you cocksucking rat-assed motherfucker. Kiss my ass." ("Eat shit, you rat-faced son of a bitch. Kiss my ass.") *(Wait for laugh to calm down.)* Milk or lemon?

JOLSON. *(With a handshake.)* Deal.

ERLE. You see, Jolie, I never in my life met a white man who let himself have as much fun as you do. I didn't think there was one till you came along. I'd be so sad if you spoiled it. It's what made me love you.

JOLSON. I love you, too. How's your day been?

ERLE. Well I had a nice visit from Oona.

JOLSON. Oona?

ERLE. You know, Charlie Chaplin's new missus. She's so sweet. And we have so much in common. She's only nineteen, but she's very mature.

JOLSON. What do you girls find to talk about?

ERLE. Well, it seems that Charlie is very sturdy, as well. She's going to have a baby.

JOLSON. *(Beat.)* That you can do with your next husband.

ERLE. Oh, and what next husband is that?

JOLSON. How should I know, I won't be around to meet him.

ERLE. Your poppa's still going at ninety-four and I expect as much from you.

JOLSON. I was just teasing. This cake is delicious.

ERLE. Momma always makes it on Daddy's birthday. It's his favorite. Jolie, what's the matter?

JOLSON. I can't remember my mama ever making a cake. I think she would have liked you.

ERLE. Me? A *shisskuh*?

JOLSON. It's *shiksa*. I don't know if she'd have cared. But guess what? I'd have married you anyway.

ERLE. Neither of our poppas was too pleased.

JOLSON. At least mine's used to it. Years ago, he asked me how could I kiss a *mezuzah* and a *shiksa* with the same mouth. I knew he was right, so I stopped kissin' *mezuzahs*. Oy, that reminds me, the guy who's playin' poppa is a joke. He's about as Jewish as Jimmy Stewart.

ERLE. I guess my ten minutes are up.

JOLSON. I'm sorry. My lips are zipped.

ERLE. Jolie, talk all you want about the picture. I think it's great they're making it and I hope it's a big hit.

JOLSON. You think it's got a chance with the kids your age?

ERLE. It's real smart of Mr. Stoloff to do swing arrangements of your old songs. They'll catch on all over again.

JOLSON. Ya think?

ERLE. And all the GIs you entertained? They'll buy your records.

JOLSON. Baby, listen. Come with me to the studio next week. I'm test recording a number for Decca and I'd love you to be there.

ERLE. That'd be great fun, Jolie. I haven't seen you perform since the day we met.

JOLSON. I'll remember that when they shove the mike in my face.

(Lights fade. When they return JOLSON is in a recording booth singing into a mic and ERLE sits in front watching.)

JOLSON. *(Sings.)*
GIMME, GIMME, GIMME, WHAT I CRY FOR
YOU KNOW YOU GOT THE BRAND OF KISSES THAT I DIE
    FOR
YOU KNOW YOU MADE ME LOVE YOU!

(ERLE applauds. JOLSON steps out of the booth.)

JOLSON. On the level baby, how was I?
ERLE. You were wonderful! You are wonderful!
JOLSON. Yeah, we'll see what Stoloff says.
STOLOFF. *(Entering.)* Jolie, that's a keeper. Terrific! Hello, Erle.
ERLE. Hi, Mr. Stoloff. I just love that arrangement.
STOLOFF. Thank you. The best players in Los Angeles signed on for this gig. There might be one little section I'd like to redo.
JOLSON. Where was that, Morris?
STOLOFF. Let's listen to the playback and see what you think. *(Shouting off.)* Cue it, Rocco.

(JOLSON's taped voice comes over the speakers. As they listen they talk.)

ERLE. It sounds so real.
STOLOFF. Best fidelity on earth. If only people could hear music this way in their homes.
JOLSON. Why? They'd stop going out. Hey, I'm Larry Parks.

(He lip-synchs broadly.)

STOLOFF. Right here, Jolie! Listen.
JOLSON. Yeah, what sounds mushy?
STOLOFF. It's the new arrangement, Jolie. You need to hold back a little to match the syncopation in the saxes.
JOLSON. I don't wanna hold back, Morris. Can't they follow me?
STOLOFF. Not without losing the swing feel.
JOLSON. Don't ask me to disappoint my audience, Morris.
STOLOFF. You're going to have a new audience, Jolie. You need to learn their kind of music.
JOLSON. You're telling me what I have to learn?!! Do you know how long I've been in this business? Do you know how long I've been singing this song?!!!
STOLOFF. Well, that's the problem....

(JOLSON reacts angrily.)

ERLE. Gentlemen, if you'll excuse me, I fixed up a thermos of some tea with honey Jolie likes for his voice, and I left it in the car. Lemme just go get it. *(Going, she "trips" and deliberately tears her shoe.)* Oh, for heaven's sake, I broke a strap! Mr. Stoloff, could I ask you a big favor? Would you mind getting it? It always makes Jolie feel so good... You know the Bentley.

(He goes.)

JOLSON. You didn't hurt yourself, did ya?

ERLE. No, sweetie, I'm fine.

JOLSON. All you hillbillies look better barefoot anyway.

ERLE. More natural, huh? Jolie, you weren't getting ready to show him your bankbook, were you?

JOLSON. Why would I do a thing like that?

ERLE. It's just an expression. Mr. Stoloff is a big fan of yours, honey, and I wouldn't want you to lose the benefit of his enthusiasm.

JOLSON. He's a dime a dozen.

ERLE. Actually I think he earns a much higher figure. You heard what he said about the caliber of the orchestra. Those men are here because they respect him, and they respect you even more. You're a legend to them, and you wouldn't want to disappoint them any more than you would your audience, or me.

JOLSON. So?

ERLE. So I'd remember that a lot has changed since the recordings you made in the thirties—

JOLSON. I don't like him pushing me around. And I don't like you pushing me around.

ERLE. I'm just trying to be helpful.

JOLSON. You think I don't know what I'm doing?!!!

ERLE. Who said anything—

JOLSON. And stop mothering me all the time!

ERLE. Jolie!

JOLSON. You can do that with your next husband—

ERLE. Stop it.

JOLSON. —and sit home nursing babies!

ERLE. Well that next husband better know how to control his temper.

JOLSON. You want out.

ERLE. I do not want out! I want you. Just stop reminding me that some day I may be alone!

JOLSON. Baby, you don't know how hard it is to be alone!

ERLE. Jolie, honey. Please—

JOLSON. You gotta learn how. You gotta start young.

ERLE. Some things, it's better to unlearn.

JOLSON. It's too late for that.

ERLE. It most surely is not. You can do anything. We can do anything.

JOLSON. I'm scared.

ERLE. Of what?

(Underscore: Sabbath hymn.)

JOLSON. "Sing so you wouldn't be scared."

ERLE. Jolie?

JOLSON. Everybody goes. No matter what you do, you lose them.

ERLE. You will never lose me. Never.

JOLSON. If I did it would kill me.

ERLE. You won't. *(Embracing each other.)* Thinking about it is one of those dumb mistakes you said you didn't want to make.

STOLOFF. *(Returning.)* I couldn't find a thermos. Maybe the trunk?

ERLE. *(Rummaging in her bag.)* Oh silly me, it's been in my bag the whole time. Talk about dumb mistakes! Jolie, you ready for tea?

JOLSON. *(Sharing the private joke with her.)* Sure, baby. While you're looking in there, see if you can find a sewing kit to fix that broken strap.

STOLOFF. So what do you think, Jolie?

JOLSON. I think it don't matter what I think. Let's take another swing at the song.

STOLOFF. We don't need to do the whole thing. Just to the end of the B section.

JOLSON. Okay, Morris. Can I bring my tea into the booth?

STOLOFF. Sure. I'll cue the band.

(He goes.)

ERLE. That's the spirit.

JOLSON. *(Heading into the booth.)* I have something to say to you, young lady. Listen closely.

(The taped intro plays and he begins to sing.)

YOU MADE ME LOVE YOU
I DIDN'T WANNA DO IT
DIDN'T WANNA DO IT
YOU MADE ME WANT YOU
AND I'LL THE TIME YOU KNEW IT
I GUESS YOU ALWAYS KNEW IT.
YOU MADE ME HAPPY SOMETIMES
YOU MADE ME GLAD—

(She crosses to the window, presses herself into it. They kiss through the glass. Lights fade and return on JOLSON at the table with BARRY.)

BARRY. I guess it would be fair to say that now your life is more exciting than ever.

JOLSON. So how come that guy in the third row fell asleep? Hey you! Wake up!

BARRY. We all know what a success *The Jolson Story* was, four Oscar nominations, including Best Actor for Larry Parks—

JOLSON. Who?

BARRY. —but I'd like to ask what the picture meant to you personally.

JOLSON. That's a big question, Barry. I dunno, I guess it meant ... I guess it meant I was still somebody. But here's a story. After the first preview in Santa Barbara, there was a couple of ladies talking about it in the lobby, and one of them says, "Isn't it a shame that Jolson didn't live to see this?"

BARRY. And what can you tell us about the sequel you're here to promote, *Jolson Sings Again*?

JOLSON. They coulda called it *Parks Lip-synchs Again*. But seriously, I think it's a terrific picture, as good as the first one, go see it. And if we make a third, I promise you I'll play me.

BARRY. And it takes your life story up to the present.

JOLSON. Almost. It doesn't mention that Erle and I now have a coupla kids. Our son, Al Jr., we adopted a year and a half ago, and just a coupla months ago our baby daughter ... Alicia.

BARRY. Congratulations. How do you like becoming a poppa so late in life?

JOLSON. Outa this world. Those kids are the best audience I ever had. Little Al, he's just twenty-two months and already he recognizes my voice over the radio.

BARRY. You think your kids will ever get to see you back on stage?

JOLSON. Until a couple days ago, Barry, I would have said no. Now I'm not so sure. My wife and I went to see an old friend who's back on Broadway after a long, what's the word?

BARRY. Hiatus?

JOLSON. Yeah. I don't want to repeat a private conversation, but it got me wondering. Getting older is like that. I never did like guys who think too much, now here I am turning into one.

(A stellar dressing room slides on. A torrent of blonde curls cascades down the back of a purple satin dressing gown as JOLSON walks in.)

MAE. *(Turning.)* Jolie! *(Rising to hug him.)* Jolie! Crawl to me, baby.

JOLSON. Hiya, Mae. Listen, you were terrific, just terrific!

MAE. I heard you were in the house, Jolie. I turned up the heat in honor of my first coach.

JOLSON. I loved your curtain speech. "Catherine the Great had over a thousand lovers ..."

MAE. "I do the best I can in two hours."

JOLSON. That was funny, Mae. Your timing, your phrasing, class all the way. And you look great. If you were a man, I'd hate you.

MAE. Where's your wife, Jolie? I'd like to meet her.

JOLSON. She had to call her mama in Arkansas. She'll be up in a few.

MAE. They say she's beautiful.

JOLSON. She loved the show, Mae. And she couldn't get over that I knew you back when.

MAE. How much did you tell her?

JOLSON. Now, Mae, so many memories have been swept down the river of time...

MAE. Yeah, and I got a broom for the rest of 'em. It's okay, Jolie, there were coaches after you.

JOLSON. I'll bet you taught 'em plenty.

MAE. Nobody ever complained. You've been to the altar a few times.

JOLSON. Four.

MAE. Four! Wedding bells must sound like an alarm clock to you.

JOLSON. The first three were just rehearsals. This time it's Run-of-the-Play.

MAE. And you got a penthouse all your own on top of the Hit Parade, more popular than ever.

JOLSON. Yeah, not bad for an *alter kocker*. It's funny, I'm not always so good with people one at a time, but give 'em to me in a crowd and I love 'em to bits.

MAE. Sure, why not? They love you right back, then they go home, and you never hear a squawk about grocery money or bladder control.

JOLSON. Erle and me are doing great.

MAE. I'm glad for you, Jolie. The Bible says a good woman is worth her weight in rubies. Of course, diamonds are a different story.

JOLSON. So, how was it, Mae? Being a real movie star?

MAE. Now, now, Jolie, you had your moment. Had quite a few, as I recall.

JOLSON. Thanks, Mae, but you know what I mean. You went the whole distance.

MAE. Timing, Jolie, that was it. The talkies were up on their feet by the time I got to 'em. You were like Christopher Columbus. You opened up a whole new world, but you thought it was someplace it wasn't.

JOLSON. Dat's deep, Mae. I'm gonna have to tink about dat one.

MAE. Well, I'm a deep kinda gal. I try to look at things from every angle. Call me Magellan.

JOLSON. I would if I could pronounce it.

MAE. The movies made me rich, Jolie, both of us rich, but there's one thing about 'em that ain't so hot. All those people who love you, they ain't in the room with you.

JOLSON. They were in the old days.

MAE. Old days, my million-dollar ass! I'm doin' it now. Whyn'cha get back on the stage?

JOLSON. Thank you, Mae. I may not look it, but I'm just a few years older than you.

MAE. I bet you're still a live one.

JOLSON. Why don't I just offer you a serenade, my sweet?

MAE. As long as the key is congenial.

Song: *April Showers*

JOLSON. *(Sings.)*
LIFE IS NOT A HIGHWAY
STREWN WITH FLOWERS
STILL IT HAS A RESERVOIR OF
    BLISS
WHEN THE SUN GIVES WAY
TO APRIL SHOWERS
HERE'S THE POINT
WE SHOULD NEVER MISS
THOUGH APRIL SHOWERS
MAY COME YOUR WAY
THEY BRING THE FLOWERS
THAT BLOOM IN MAY
SO IF IT'S RAININ'
HAVE NO REGRETS
BECAUSE IT ISN'T RAINING RAIN
YOU KNOW
IT'S RAININ' VIOLETS
AND WHEN YOU SEE CLOUDS
UPON THE HILL
YOU SOON WILL SEE CROWDS
OF DAFFODILS
SO KEEP ON LOOKING
FOR THE BLUEBIRD
AND LISTENING FOR HIS SONG
WHENEVER APRIL SHOWERS
COME ALONG

MAE. *(Speaks in response.)*
You can say that again.

That's French, right?

Oh, lay it on me Jolie….

Don't bring them showers my way.

Oh. I'm bloomin'.

I never regret a thing.

Oh, flowers.
Where? Where?
Don't bring those clouds down here.

I love the crowds.

Tweet, tweet.

JOLSON. Is the key congenial, Miss West?
MAE. Let's give it a try and see.

JOLSON. *(Sings.)*
THOUGH APRIL SHOWERS
MAY COME YOUR WAY
THEY BRING THE FLOWERS
THAT BLOOM IN MAY

MAE. *(Sings in response.)*
I'VE KNOWN A FEW
YOU BEAUTIFUL JEW
I'M CRAZY FOR YOU
WE MAKE A BEAUTIFUL
    TWO

MAE. *(Sings.)*
SO IF ITS RAININ'
HAVE NO REGRETS

BECAUSE IT ISN'T RAININ'
RAIN

JOLSON. *(Sings in response.)*
HOW I LOVED YOU IN THE RAIN
AND NOW TO BE WITH YOU
AGAIN
I'M THIRTY AGAIN
I KNOW

BOTH.
IT'S RAININ' VIOLETS

JOLSON. *(Sings.)*
AND WHEN YOU SEE CLOUDS
UPON THE HILL
YOU SOON WILL SEE CROWDS
OF DAFFODILS

MAE. *(Sings in response.)*
NOT A CLOUD IN THE SKY
TILL THE DAY I DIE
NOT A TEAR IN MY EYE
IT'S CAUSE I LOVE YA
THAT'S WHY

BOTH.
SO KEEP ON LOOKING FOR THE BLUEBIRD
AND LISTENING FOR HIS SONG
WHENEVER APRIL SHOWERS COME ALONG.

(Slow fade. BARRY meets JOLSON center stage.)

BARRY. So you may yet come back to Broadway?

JOLSON. I don't know, Barry. The shows today are so different from the stuff I used to do. But I'll tell you one thing, if this country ever goes to war again, which I hope we don't, anywhere they send the boys, I'm there on my own tab. And I'll come back here any time you want me.

BARRY. Thank you, Al. Shall we say goodnight then?

JOLSON. You say it. I've got a big lump in my throat and I think I'll just go home and swallow it.

BARRY. Al Jolson, it's been a real pleasure.

JOLSON. All mine.

BARRY. As the Irish say, *Sholom aleichem.* Wanna sing us off?

JOLSON. You know, Barry, in honor of this great old theater, and all the folks who've filled it, I could sing again, only for old times' sake let's do it off mic.

BARRY. That's a nice idea, Al, but don't forget the million people listening at home.

JOLSON. Tell 'em to open their windows.

Song: *You Made Me Love You* (Finale)

JOLSON. *(Sings.)*
YOU MADE ME LOVE YOU,
I DIDN'T WANNA DO IT,
I DIDN'T WANNA DO IT,
I WANT SOME LOVE THAT'S TRUE
YES, I DO, 'NDEED I DO, DON'T YOU?
GIMME, GIMME, GIMME, GIMME WHAT I CRY FOR
YOU GOT IT...
GOT THE LOVIN' I DIE FOR
YOU KNOW YOU MADE ME LOVE YOU!

CURTAIN

PROPERTY LIST

Prop	Top of show preset
Note cards	SL prop shelf
Pitcher with water	Onstage: SL desk
2 water glasses	Onstage: SL desk
Mic on table stand	Onstage: SL desk
Small table	Onstage: SL
2 chairs	Onstage: SL
Bedding for Momma	US pallet: bed
Headboard for Momma	US pallet: bed
Bed	US pallet
2 pillows	US pallet
Black book	SL prop shelf
Coin	Personal
Black towel	SL prop shelf
Makeup box	SL prop shelf
Beat-up chair	USL storage
Coat rack	USL storage
Beat-up dressing table	USL storage
Sheet music (Stephen Foster-esque)	SR pallet: on chair
Fancy chair	SR pallet
Fancy music stand	SR pallet
Large, nice dressing table	USL storage
Water glass with water	SL prop shelf
Bentwood chair	USL storage
Mirror with lights	SL hallway
Sheet music	SL prop shelf
Telegrams	SL hall: on mirror
Blackface jar	SL prop shelf: makeup box
Flask	SR quick change
Metal chair	SR. storage
Director's chair	USR storage
Purse	SL prop shelf
Cigarettes (unfiltered Lucky Strikes)	SL prop shelf: purse
Lighter	SL prop shelf: purse
Cigarette case	SL prop shelf: purse
Compact with mirror and puff	SL prop shelf: purse
Teddy bear	SR prop shelf
Child's bed	DSR storage

Prop	**Top of show preset**
Patio loveseat	USR storage
Patio table	USR storage
Plant in square pot	USR storage
Medium dressing table	USR storage
Large envelope with papers	SL prop shelf
Radio script pages	SR prop shelf
Folding chair	USR storage
Square mic on floor stand	USR storage
Paper coffee cup with water	SR prop shelf
Bankbook	Personal (Jolson)
Military-style desk	USL storage
Plain black phone	SL prop shelf
Pad and pen	SL prop shelf
Hotel phone table	USR storage
Princess phone	SR prop shelf
Poofy chair	USR storage
Orchid in fancy pot	USR storage
Wrapped daisies	SR prop shelf
Purse	SR prop shelf
Wide medical tape	SL: in hospital table
Hospital side table	SL prop shelf
Folding screen	USL storage
Vase	SL prop shelf
IV bottle with tube	SL prop shelf
Hospital bedding	USL storage
Hospital headboard and footboard	SL prop shelf
Thermos with cup	SR prop shelf: in purse
Fancier black phone	SL prop shelf
Cigar	SL prop shelf
2 rocks glasses with water and fake ice cubes	SR prop shelf
2 small plants	USR storage
2 deck chairs	USR storage
Deck table	USR storage
Oscar^{TM} statuette	SR prop shelf
Cake serving plate	SR prop shelf
Sugar tongs	SR prop shelf
Cake plate	SR prop shelf
Serving knife	SR prop shelf

Prop	**Top of show preset**
Napkin (A)	SR prop shelf
Teacup, saucer and teaspoon (A)	SR prop shelf
Teapot with tea	SR prop shelf
Creamer with milk	SR prop shelf
Sugar bowl with cubes	SR prop shelf
Fork	SR prop shelf
Cake (yellow jelly roll)	SR prop shelf
Café table	SL hallway
2 café chairs	SL hallway
2 plants in round pots	SL hallway
Napkin (B)	SR prop shelf
Teacup, saucer and teaspoon (B)	SR prop shelf
Rocks glass with tea	SR prop shelf
Studio window/bench unit	USR storage
Silver studio mic on stand	USR storage
You Made Me Love You sheet music	SL prop shelf
2 vases of flowers	SL prop shelf
Fancy mirror	SL hallway
Boa	SL hallway
Chair for Mae	SL hallway
Skirt for Mae's table	SL prop shelf

SCROOGE!

BOOK, MUSIC AND LYRICS BY
Leslie Bricusse

"Wonderful theatre."
Yorkshire Evening Post

"Sensational.... It was terrific."
BBC Radio

"Just wait until you see *Scrooge!*"
Radio 3 – Australia

This is the wildly successful stage version of the classical movie musical based on *A Christmas Carol* which starred Albert Finney. Adapted by a renowned writer-composer-lyricist, it is an easy-to-produce show to delight audiences during the holiday season. CD available. (#21029)

Sanders Family Christmas

WRITTEN BY	**CONCEIVED BY**
Connie Ray	Alan Bailey

MUSICAL ARRANGEMENTS BY
John Foley & Gary Fagin

From the creators of the
"perfectly delightful,"[1] "totally beguiling,"[2]
"charming and funny"[3] musical comedy
SMOKE ON THE MOUNTAIN

It's December 24, 1941, and America is going to war. So is Dennis Sanders of the Sanders Family Singers. Join Pastor Mervin Oglethorpe and the memorable Sanders family as they evoke some down-home Christmas cheer with hilarious, touching stories and 25 bluegrass Christmas songs. Here is a richly entertaining musical that has audiences clapping, stomping and singing along with the *SMOKE ON THE MOUNTAIN* crowd. (#20948)

Send for your copy of the Samuel French
BASIC CATALOGUE OF PLAYS AND MUSICALS

THE ORIGINAL
SANDERS FAMILY MUSICAL HIT

Smoke on the Mountain

BOOK BY   **CONCEIVED BY**
Connie Ray   Alan Bailey

MUSICAL ARRANGEMENTS BY
Mike Craver & Mark Hardwick

"Perfectly delightful"
The New Yorker

"A charming and funny celebration of America"
The New York Times

"Totally beguiling …Not to be missed"
New York Post

"A sophisticated audience went simply wild"
Philadelphia Daily News

"A rollicking blend of monologues and musical numbers"
Variety

The year is 1938. It's Saturday night in Mount Pleasant, North Carolina, (home of the Mount Pleasant Pickle Factory) and the Reverend Oglethorpe has invited the Sanders Family Singers to provide an up-liftin' evening of singin' and witnessin'. The audience is invited to pull up a pew and join the congregation for a rollicking good time. More than two dozen songs, many of them vintage pop hymns, and hilarious stories from the more or less devout Sanders family members provide a richly entertaining experience that is evocative of another era. 4 m., 3 f. (#21236)